SUCCEED!

AN INSPIRATIONAL TOOLKIT FOR THE SERIOUS ENTREPRENEUR

IHQLAK HUSSAIN

DISCLAIMER

Whilst I have exclusively designed this book for you to utilise for your business, I cannot guarantee the accuracy or completeness of any information which is contained here and in no circumstances shall be liable for any loss or damage suffered as a result of relying upon it.

DEDICATION

First of all, I dedicate this book to the memories of my late father (Haji Karamat Hussain) and late grandfather (Faroz Khan). Two people who have been very instrumental in my development.
This is also for my mum, children and long-suffering wife; they light up my life in so many ways.

For my team at AMCI, a leader without a loyal team can only go so far. I appreciate all that you do.

Finally, this book would not have been possible without the advice and editing of my dear colleague and friend – Prof. Melvyn Pryer, Director of the International Centre at University College Birmingham, UK (formerly the dean of two schools – The Business School and The School of Recreation, Sport and Tourism). I would also like to take this opportunity to thank the team at Discover Your Bounce Publishing for all the support provided in bringing this book to fruition. Thank you all so much.

For those that always wanted to start business but did not know how to do it. Here is the road to your financial freedom!

SUCCEED!

FOREWORD
BY PROFESSOR MELVYN PRYER

Being your own boss holds appeal to many, eager to escape existing draconian work places, provide personalised services or as a positive alternative to redundancy, with would-be entrepreneurs eager to follow business dreams. It is perhaps not surprising that start-up business ventures have emerged as key drivers of economic growth and job creation, and are often a catalyst for radical innovation. Indeed, 'young' firms account for about 20% of employment but create almost half of new jobs on average across OECD countries, and with innovation by young firms now contributing significantly to aggregate productivity growth (OECD, 2016).

Even amid the economic gloom of the Covid-19 crisis— recession, unemployment, and business failures— there exists the realisation that entrepreneurial opportunities may arise, for such crises create problems that people need solutions to and start-up business ventures are clamouring to cure. However, significant challenges exist in the business start-up environment amongst those eager to seek out short-run and longer-run opportunities, which this book seeks to redress.

As someone who had developed their own business as a copywriter after leaving university and who has subsequently advised others on starting a new venture, I can appreciate both the opportunities and challenges faced in a business start-up. In my own case I was simply referred to a book on tax as the basis for starting a business venture which left me woefully unprepared in regards to keeping plans and records and in seeking new business expansion opportunities.

In many ways, I resembled the students I was to teach at university in the future, who were vocationally orientated and who possessed basic accounting and marketing knowledge, but who had little idea where to really start with a business plan.

I first met Ihqlak Hussain at University College Birmingham where we both taught graduate students in fields such as hospitality, food, tourism, beauty and leisure management. Many elected to take an optional module in Business Enterprise, as they aspired to a future in running their own venture. Yet, as with many new entrepreneurs, while our students were typically full of ideas, they needed guidance in developing and organising their thoughts into comprehensive business plans, particularly in regards to the finance related aspects.

Accordingly, this book is derived from the gem of a handout that Ihqlak produced at University College Birmingham some twenty years ago to address the challenge of simplifying business plans for non-business students. Ihqlak's handout was continually refined over the years and grew ever more sophisticated, developing into a booklet, before eventually becoming the basis of a well-received degree in Business Enterprise. Furthermore, the 'Start-Up' booklet was to become an aide-memoir of guidance to all of our teaching team involved in advising on business start-ups, underpinned an EU funded project to promote start-up ventures and was borrowed by other institutions who recognised effective practice at work. As is shown in this book, the aim was to produce an easily followed template towards producing a workable business plan.

With over twenty years' experience in business start-ups, through university lecturing and in client consultations at AMCI, Ihqlak is ideally qualified to advise on business start-ups. His straightforward guidance to entrepreneurs has covered start-ups of various scales in many sectors throughout the peaks and troughs of the economic climate. Today, the business environment may be uncertain, but for agile entrepreneurs with an appetite for innovation, now could be the time to start a business of your own. So use this book and don't rule out becoming your own boss to meet your own business dreams!

CONTENTS

SUCCEED!

MY STORY

I was born in Birmingham, United Kingdom to immigrant parents of Pakistani origin. They came to the UK after World War Two, to help rebuild Britain and improve their own fortunes in the process. Dad progressed well on the production floor, becoming a precision Engineer and after a few years in the UK amassed sufficient savings to start a business back in Pakistan. A common theme for many who originally came from an Indian sub-continent, until the late seventies, was to save up, and return back to their home country. My family decided to return to Pakistan when I was three years old, in 1973.

Dad purchased some land to set up a rice plantation business near Lahore (Capital of Culture in Pakistan)—a day away from our hometown of Dadyal, in the Mirpur district. Since Dad was focused on the business, Mum had to raise all five of us largely on her own in the village of Kandore in Dadyal—no easy task. This was particularly difficult as we were born in the UK and used to a certain degree of luxury that could not be easily replicated in a village in Pakistan. Schooling was fairly basic and only in Urdu; life was in the slow lane. The business, whilst having early successes, was only making modest gains. Dad had left his inexperienced partners in charge and returned back to UK a few years after starting the venture. Dad had a great deal of responsibility on his shoulders as the eldest of three siblings and felt that his personality and skills were better suited to life in the UK than Pakistan and the economy was more attractive. At the same time he felt that we would have a better life in the village!

Dad and his partners were resilient and kept the business afloat with Dad's financial support from the UK for a number of years, eventually selling the business for a profit in the late seventies. After spending nearly eight years in Pakistan, during the seventies, Mum managed to convince Dad to bring us back home to Birmingham in September 1981. By now, Dad had done reasonably well in comparison with many of his contemporaries by landing a good job on the production floor with GKN Plc. He had purchased a large Tudor style home for us in Handsworth, Birmingham—close to his work place in Hamstead, Birmingham.

Whilst home was close to Dad's workplace, it was not an ideal place to bring up children. Located in an area with high unemployment, especially amongst large immigrant communities. This led to a lot of petty crime, violence (Handsworth Riots in 1986 being a prime example), and a lot of criminal activities associated with drugs. This was largely driven by initially West Indian gangs and then subsequently gangs of Indian sub-continent heritage, based in and around the area. Dad inspired us to work hard at school—advice we did not always follow, possibly due to bad social influences and poor schooling. Teachers focused their attention more on controlling the unruly classrooms and less on teaching—they clearly had their work cut out.

I was initially excited to attend school to learn English and make new friends, in my birth country—England. Whilst I made friends, the only time we really tried to speak English was in front of the teachers during the classes, as the majority of children had English as their second language and preferred to speak in their own mother tongues the rest of the time. This adversely affected our learning but allowed me to make friends easily as I had no exposure to the English language before returning to the UK. As a result, I left school with just two C grade GCSEs. During the summer that year, Dad helped me to get a job in his friend's savoury snacks factory (I kept that job for three weeks and gained enough experience to last a life time). I tried my hand at being a waiter in an Indian restaurant and literally burnt my fingertips in the process. The owner expected us to carry hot balti woks without any protection to impress his Caucasian customers. I left that job after two weeks and became a cashier/shop assistant at a supermarket.

After the summer was over that year, I realised that I needed to get away from friends and the local influences by enrolling at a college that was nearly an hour away on the bus. No one really knew who I was—a fresh start was what I felt was so desperately needed. I believed I could do better and how right I was. After the first year on the Business and Finance course, I passed with a distinction. The college awarded me a prize at a ceremony held at the famous Birmingham Symphony Hall for the overall best achieving student of the year. Since then I have never looked back, I have worked hard—always giving 100%. I adopted a positive attitude to life, remained committed and believed in my ability to Succeed!

Fast-forward to 1997, when I qualified as a Chartered Certified Accountant, with first-time passes in my professional exams with the Association of Chartered Certified Accountants (ACCA). No easy task for a boy that could not even read, write or speak any word of English until the age of eleven. Along with university lecturing in business and management programmes nationally and globally, I founded AMCI in 2003. I set this business up as a specialised 'one-stop shop', boutique accountancy, taxation and business advisory services firm. We have clients exclusively from the small and medium-sized business sector and taxpayers throughout the UK and beyond. Business growth has been such that I had committed myself full-time to AMCI by 2015.

AMCI has been assisting our clients with high quality accountancy, taxation and business advisory services for over seventeen years and we are a relentlessly client-focused firm. What makes us unique and highly trusted is not just the 'one-stop shop' approach, but also the care and attention provided to all our clients. The AMCI business approach lies in offering clients a specialised service, akin to outsourcing their finance department—with significant cost savings!

As a leader, I believe we have been helping entrepreneurs to create a business on purpose rather than by chance so that they can succeed. I wanted to make a difference and feel we surely do at AMCI. Ninety-eight percent of these businesses have succeeded by adopting our tried and tested formulae since 2003. Take a look below at what some of our clients and partners are saying about us.

We are also committed to being a socially responsible corporate citizen and as a result, donate 10 percent of our profits to good causes with a focus on social enterprise activities in vulnerable communities. I feel it is important to share our successes with those that are less fortunate than us who have the desire and hunger to succeed—just like me at an earlier point in my career.

When not advising clients, I enjoy travelling, having visited many countries and cultures throughout Europe, Africa and Asia including the Indian-subcontinent. I also enjoy taking morning walks in the park and spending time with family including my adorable grandchildren—Safa and Yousuf.

SUCCEED!

CLIENTS

Ian Allen (High Growth UK Start-Up with International Aspirations)

Ihqlak has been advising us from the start of our entrepreneurial journey for nearly ten years. Without his sound advice on cash flow management, profitability and business development, we would not have become a multi-million pound business within a short period of time. He is truly the father of our business and we cannot thank him enough and his team for all the support given. The team at AMCI is currently advising us on our international venture.

Irfan Lal (High Growth Serial Entrepreneur)

My company—Floors Direct Midlands Ltd. has been with AMCI for almost ten years. They are very efficient and reliable. They take care of all my accounts, from payroll, VAT, corporation tax, tax investigations to consultancy. AMCI have greatly assisted me in expanding my business empires, consisting of online flooring products business, shops and warehouses, a property portfolio, restaurant and storage businesses. Furthermore, in having to deal with the ever-demanding HMRC, I would highly recommend AMCI to you!

Clare Hitchens (Head to Toe Beauty)

Without your help Ihqlak, I could not have got the business started. You and your team are absolutely amazing!

Paul Upton (A1 Top Job Roofing Services Ltd.)

Thank you for advising us over many years, your support has been immensely appreciated.

Saju Sekher (Contractor)

As a beginner, the advice I had from Ihqlak and his team was very valuable. I had the opportunity to have a meeting with Ihqlak before setting up my business and he took the time to explain about the accounts process and other formalities. I started my company in 2014 and since then I have had an excellent service from the team and they have always been very professional and prompt with all the returns and other paperwork. They have always taken extra care to support my business and one thing I have always appreciated is the quick response I get from them regarding any queries I raise and this includes any references my business required from the accountant. There have been instances when the team at AMCI has worked out of business hours to help me. I have recommended the firm to many of my colleagues and will continue to do so.

John Smith (High Growth Start-Up Enterprise)

Highly recommend AMCI. They have helped us so much with so many aspects of our business. I couldn't do without them. We are really grateful for all their help.

Jassy Rai (Entrepreneur and Property Investor)

I have been with AMCI for over ten years now and like previous reviewers have said, the service is first class. Ihqlak is very experienced in his field and equally as knowledgeable and is backed up by a very effective team. Nothing is too much trouble. I would not go anywhere else. Keep up the good work!

David Walton (Freelance Services International)

Ihqlak's advice and help has been invaluable. His understanding of international markets has greatly assisted me to develop my business despite the Brexit debacle.

Saleem Sattar (Professional Services and Catering Businesses)

I have worked with AMCI since I qualified as a pharmacist and cannot rate their services highly enough. Ihqlak is very knowledgeable, professional and thorough. I have total peace of mind knowing he is dealing with all the 'nitty gritty' details of my accounts. That's not all, AMCI are very proactive in chasing me if I am late (sorry Ihqlak) and genuinely care to ensure I have my affairs in order to give the complete package of a personal and professional service. Thanks Ihqlak.

PARTNERS

Vikul Gupta (Director – Creative Info Tech Ltd.)

Over the years, I have worked very closely with the team at AMCI in finding IT solutions for their clients, particularly in the creation of websites and devising online strategies for small businesses. I have found Ihqlak and his team at AMCI very proactive in assisting their clients.

Arun Chauhan (Director – Tenet Law)

I have had the pleasure of working with Ihqlak at AMCI Associates on a few occasions. He has a great eye for detail, is very user and client friendly. He works thoroughly on the cases we have been involved in to add insight and value for clients.

Mohammed Zafar (Managing Partner – Equity Solicitors)

I have known Ihqlak for well over fifteen years and advised him and some of his clients on all aspects of property matters from a legal perspective. Ihqlak and his team at AMCI are relentlessly client focused and therefore, always a pleasure to work with. I would not hesitate in recommending them for property tax advice and planning.

Matt Timby FCCA (Director - Randd UK Limited)

We first met Ihqlak at the AAT Annual Accountancy conference a few years ago now, and we got on so well we've been doing business with him ever since, achieving a 100 percent success rate on research and development credits. We've always found Ihqlak to be a down-to-earth and a 'no nonsense' accountant and business advisor, straight to the point and gets the job done, whilst remaining professional at all times. He's very close to his clients and we can see that he treats them as part of the AMCI family. We have no hesitation in recommending AMCI for your accountancy, tax, and business advice.

SUCCEED!

1 BUSINESS START-UP

'Someone's sitting in the shade today because someone planted a tree a long time ago.'

Warren Buffett – Investor, one of the world's richest people.

'Finding something frustrating and seeing an opportunity to make it better is what entrepreneurship is all about.'

Richard Branson – The Virgin Group

Since the start of 2020, we have been living in unprecedented times. From the onset of Covid-19 in March, to the great deal of remaining uncertainty caused by Brexit, we are all facing the most challenging times of our lifetime.

Supermarkets and wholesalers have been warning shoppers of fresh produce shortages. This is due to bans imposed by our European neighbours on hauliers carrying freight across the Channel in an effort to contain the spread of the virus. According to news sources retailers expect shelves could soon be empty of some fresh produce imported from Europe. This means preparation is key. In a start-up, regardless of the challenges in the business environment, preparation and sound advice from trusted experts is the key to success.

Whilst a deal on Brexit was reached as the clock stopped ticking on Christmas Eve in 2020, unfortunately supply chains will not be the same again in the short-term. Those of us who are reliant upon overseas produce need to order early and expect an increase in prices and further delays at the borders. What does this mean if you are looking to start in business in these unpredicted times?

Fortune favours the bold and beautiful. Fortunes are to be made in downturns; opportunities are there for some but require careful planning and sound advice. I was there with my team for our clients in the great financial crash of 2007/2008 and managed to successfully manoeuvre them to new heights. We have been doing the same again, but this time even better than before as we are more experienced with operating in difficult conditions, whether it is due to a pandemic or economic crisis. Being a relentlessly client-focused firm, our clients' interests are always a priority, especially with business start-ups.

Business start-ups are the backbone of the economy. You might then ask why are there such high failure rates nationally? There are a number of reasons for this, such as ill-conceived ideas, poor advice or lack of it. In addition, small businesses often fail due to a lack of capital or funding, faulty infrastructure or business model, inadequate management team or poor/unsuccessful marketing strategies. This book looks at all of these areas in detail and shows you how costly mistakes can be avoided to allow your business to succeed!

Some of us are destined to be entrepreneurs. From a young age, we have the fire in our belly to start a business and lead it to success, like Sir Richard Branson. Failure is not an option when you are totally committed to the cause. For others, it is a very scary journey as there are so many unknown variables to deal with. If you are looking to take the plunge, the benefits of flexibility, playing by your own rules, pursuing your passions and ultimately gaining financial freedom awaits.

Whilst nationally business failure rates are incredibly high, especially in the current climate, I have a tried and tested formula that has led to an overall 98 percent success rate for all of our start-up clients since 2003. This book has been exclusively designed to assist you to thoroughly plan, develop and execute a new business venture. I have been advising start-ups since 2003 with a great deal of success. I hope that you will find this book useful in formulating a plan of action for your business venture. If you are serious about developing your idea into a fully-fledged business, read and understand this book and use it as a road map to your financial freedom, regardless of the economic downturn.

SERIOUS HEALTH WARNING:

Starting a business is not for the faint-hearted. If you are bold, courageous and have the fire in the belly to start your own business, then read on as I will help you to gain the financial freedom that you aspire to. Alternatively, stop here or it will seriously damage your health and financial wellbeing! However, if you just wish to learn more about starting your own business in the future, continue reading. The next section is a Personality Test you might want to take before embarking on this incredible journey.

SUCCEED!

2 BUSINESS START-UP PERSONALITY TEST

'The more time you spend contemplating what you should have done…
you lose valuable time planning what you can and will do."
Lil Wayne, Rapper

'God has a plan for you. You are exactly where he wants you right now.'
Anon

So what does it take to succeed in business?

By taking this test, you will find out how suitable you are to be embarking on an exciting entrepreneurial journey. Please be completely honest in order to truly reveal your ability to start a new enterprise. Once you have completed the test, that should take you no more than ten minutes, please turn to Appendix 1 to assess the outcomes. If you are being true to yourself, do not turn to Appendix 1 until the test is fully completed. It is best to complete all of the questions in one go.

I want to control how much I make (i.e. the harder I work, the more money I make).	YES	NO
I want independence to be my own boss and have no-one to answer to but myself (and to my customers).	YES	NO
I want to have flexible working hours (i.e. I don't mind working day and night, week-ends, as long as I am the one chooses to do so).	YES	NO
I am good at making decisions	YES	NO
I want to create things.	YES	NO
I often predict trends before they happen.	YES	NO
I am the type of person who is always finding or creating opportunities.	YES	NO
When I have a good idea or notice an opportunity, I do something about it (i.e. I seize opportunities).	YES	NO
I like change and look forward to it.	YES	NO
I like to constantly improve things.	YES	NO
I have expertise, a skill, a product or service that is worth buying on the competitive market.	YES	NO
I have worked in a business like the one I want to start. I have previous experience in this industry.	YES	NO

I have a base of contacts and potential future clients who might require my services or product, enough to keep my business afloat in year one.	YES	NO
I have trustworthy contacts in the accounting and legal professions to assist me.	YES	NO
I enjoy contract-chasing, sales and negotiating, 'wheeling and dealing'.	YES	NO
I have savings or someone to financially support me through the rough spots.	YES	NO
At least for the first six months in business?	YES	NO
I have the moral support of my family or significant other.	YES	NO
I have good strong physical health.	YES	NO
I have good strong emotional health and I am able to stay enthusiastic by myself.	YES	NO
Even when the going gets tough?	YES	NO
I am willing and/or able to give up many hours of my personal life to ensure the smooth running of my business.	YES	NO
I like to work alone most of the time and I am self-reliant.	YES	NO
I am organised enough to manage my tasks and prioritise my time.	YES	NO

SUCCEED!

3 BUSINESS PLANNING

'By failing to prepare, you are preparing to fail.'
Benjamin Franklin – one of the Founding Fathers of the USA

'A man who does not plan long ahead will find trouble at his door.'
Confucius – Chinese Philosopher

All businesses, new or existing, need to conduct effective planning. Consideration must be given to all of the following:

- Is it the right time to start a venture?
- Where are you going?
- Have you got the ability to get there?
- How are you going to do it?
- How much will it cost?
- How much will you get out of it?
- Is it worthwhile?

It is of great importance that this information is written down in order to get your thinking straight. This can then be used to put ideas into action and act as a benchmark upon which progress can be monitored once the business has commenced operation. Once completed this document is known as the Business Plan.

Starting in business is a serious matter. By preparing a business plan, you will gain a deep understanding of what it will take YOUR business to SUCCEED. Your Business Plan is basically a thoroughly researched and refined document that will help you to communicate your vision, raise finance, refine your aims and objectives, and evaluate your business proposal. Therefore, it is a very valuable document that you should prepare so that you can fulfill your goals.

The Business Plan will also act as a very useful tool when trying to raise finance from either a bank or any other financial institution, as your understanding of the business will be clear to all others concerned. It will also act as a route map for your business as it grows and you should refer to it regularly to see that the business is still on track with your overall aims and objectives. The plan may change over time, which is fine, but you should always update your Business Plan to show this.

I would advise you to write the plan as if the person reading it has no prior knowledge of your business or specialist sector. If you intend to use this document to raise capital for the business venture, it is fair to say that the financier you are targeting (e.g. bank, angel investor, grant provider) may not always be an expert in your field. The more information you can give about the opportunities/markets, the greater the chance of being successful.

AMCI can assist you in consultancy advice on the business start-up, growth and development. In terms of raising finance, I can provide direct market access to lenders with highly competitive borrowing rates. Contact me.at info@amci-associates.co.uk so that I can assist you to succeed every step of the way!

4 BUSINESS PLAN TOOLKIT

'Good intentions might sound nice but it's positive actions that matter....
opportunity doesn't make appointments, you have to be ready when it
arrives.'

Tim Fargo – Entrepreneur & Keynote Speaker

'Unless commitment is made, there are only promises and hopes;
but no plans.'

Peter F Drucker – renowned Management Consultant

There are a variety of formats for business plans. As long as you cover all the sections and present the information clearly, the structure and headings are not vitally important. Indeed, I would encourage you to design models or illustrations to further emphasise any aspect of any section. Be original, imaginative, innovative and creative. Demonstrate your passion for the business, but make sure you can follow the plan you have developed!

The content of each section is your own decision and will reflect your analysis and understanding of the business planning process for your proposed business venture. The following outline contains all the relevant information that should be covered in your plan, as recommended practice by many high-street lenders and angel investors. Read on for our suggestions.

SECTION 1.   EXECUTIVE SUMMARY

'Write your executive summary of where you want to take your business, and why your business idea will be successful.'
Timi Nadela – Entrepreneur

The Executive Summary should be written once all other sections have been completed. It should be about a page in length, covering all key aspects of your business. Make it enthusiastic, professional, complete and concise. If applying for a loan, state clearly the amount required, the purpose of the loan and expected return on investment. Highlight key financial indicators graphically.

The Executive Summary should include:

- The company's mission statement and/or vision statement.
- Information about the company's owners.
- An outline of your business model.
- The target market.
- The competition and what sets you apart.
- Your sales strategies and campaigns.
- The company's current financial status, goals, projections (over at least three years), and needs.
- An implementation plan for bringing the business into the real world.
- Start-up financing requirements.

Often, this is the only section that is read by potential investors so make it count!

EXAMPLE – SUPREME BEAUTY LTD

Supreme Beauty is going to be a new retail business located on a busy high street in Handsworth, Birmingham. It will specialise in offering Afro-Caribbean and European hair and cosmetics products for beauty conscientious consumers. It will also provide foot spa and nail treatment services for its clientele. Customers will be able to book online appointments on its website and also place orders for collection of

---

supplies. Much of the business is going to be generated from Handsworth and surrounding areas. Supreme Beauty will benefit from the fact that there are no other similar businesses in the locality and a high degree of Afro-Caribbean people living in the area that currently have to travel outside the area to source the necessary supplies.

The business is going to be run by Mr Thomas Bennett and his spouse, Mrs Diane Bennett. Both have many years managerial experience. They will also employee three full-time and four part-time shop assistants as the business is planning to open seven days per week. Supreme Beauty will offer its services in a peaceful, relaxed atmosphere. It will also provide a friendly working environment, respecting creativity, inclusion and diversity.

The business will primarily source its products directly from established wholesalers from USA and China. Two main suppliers in the UK have also agreed to supply the stock on thirty days credit. All hair and cosmetic products stocked will be of a high standard and in compliance with UK safety rules and regulations.

The business needs to raise £165,000 start-up capital. Mr and Mrs Bennett will inject £90,000 from their own savings and borrow the remaining £75,000 over a ten year period. This will be used to acquire a ten year lease on a currently empty premises recently renovated with a break-out clause in year threw and five with a deposit of £8,000. Rent of £5000 will be paid quarterly in advance. Fixtures, fittings and equipment will be purchased locally costing £45,000 and investment in stock of £92,000. The remaining amount will be used for working capital purposes. Weekly sales are expected to be initially £22,150 rising by 10% per annum. The financial highlights expected are as follows for the first three years.

For more details please refer to the graphs at www.amci-associates.co.uk/succeed.

Executive Summary Outline

- Your business's mission statement and/or vision statement.
- Information about the owners of your business.
- An outline of your business model.
- The target market.
- The competition and what sets you apart.
- Your sales strategies and campaigns.
- Your business's current financial status, goals, projections (over at least three years), and needs.
- An implementation plan for bringing your business into the real world.
- Start-up financing requirements.

You can download the above template from www.amci-associates.co.uk/succeed/

SUCCEED!

SECTION 2. CONTENTS

'There's no shortage of remarkable ideas, what's missing is the will to execute them.' – *Seth Godin, Writer*

It is important to get the contents right. Make sure the contents flow well and reflect the nature of the business. Number the pages retrospectively once the business plan is completed and set out all the sections as follows:

Outline Contents

1. Executive Summary
2. Contents
3. The Business Concept
4. The Key People
5. Market Research
6. Marketing Plan and Strategy
7. Operations
8. Legal Issues
9. Finance
10. Presenting Financial Forecasts in Your Business Plan
11. Appendices– include any ancillary or any other relevant material

To present your business plan well, ensure it is designed well with your branding on each page. Take time on your presentation and get someone to edit the final document for you, as you may miss typos, etc. This document should reflect not only the detail that shows your knowledge, but also the pride you have in the business you have built.

SUCCEED!

SECTION 3.   THE BUSINESS CONCEPT

'No matter what people tell you, words and ideas can change the world.'
Robin Williams - Actor

The business concept is essentially an idea for a business that includes fundamental information such as the product or service, the target market, and the unique selling points that give the business advantages over its competitors. This can be a new product, service or a fresh approach to marketing an existing product or service.

What is the Big Idea?

Briefly explain the idea, demonstrating your enthusiasm for it. Detail its origins, where did the idea come from?

Why Do You Want to Start Your Own Business?

Consider:

Making your own decisions

Developing a business idea

Using your skills in your own business

Wanting to be your own boss, etc.

What Is The Purpose of the Business?

- Outline why you think there is a demand for the product or service? Is there a gap in the market? How do you know there is a gap?

- Identify the general idea, products or services you intend to supply.

- To whom will you market your products? (State it briefly here, you will do a more thorough explanation in the Marketing Plan sections.)

- Describe your business sector. Is it a growth industry? What changes do you foresee in the industry short-term and long-term? How will your company be poised to take advantage of them?

Describe your most important strengths and core competencies. What factors will make the company succeed? What do you think your major competitive strengths will be? What background experience, skills, and strengths do you personally bring to this new venture?

Evaluating the Opportunity

The model below can be used to evaluate your business opportunity in terms of demonstrable need and ability to generate profits. If the need for your business is high and you have the ability and potential to satisfy the need, you are on to a potential winner! Alternatively, if the demand is low, and your ability to carry it out is also low, go and invest your time elsewhere.

Type of Business

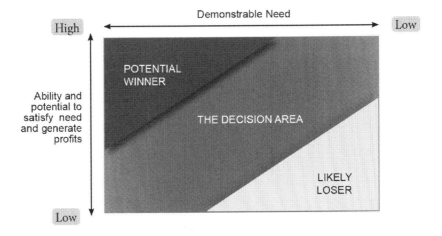

There are a number of different types of business organisation and ownership namely:

- Sole Traders.
- Partnerships.
- Limited Companies.
- Co-operatives.
- Franchises.
- Public Limited Companies.

Sole Traders

This is the simplest form of business and can be just the owner of the business or he/she may employ others. The business is owned and operated by one person and there is no distinction between that person and the organisation. The owner provides the capital and receives the profits and is personally responsible for all liabilities. Typical businesses of sole traders are plumbing, decorating, electricians, and small independent shops such as florists and barber shops.

Advantages

- It is simple to set up and dissolve.
- Few legal requirements, other than keeping a set of accounts for tax and VAT, and possibly needing to obtain a licence for certain business activities.
- Customers receive personal attention.
- Freedom to make all decisions independently.
- All profits retained by owner.

Disadvantages

- The owner has unlimited liability for business debts.
- May limit business development due to lack of managerial skills.
- Very high level of personal commitment required resulting often in very long working hours and few holidays.
- The business is reliant on one person which can be problematic if the owner is ill or away.
- A very small business is vulnerable to competition.

Partnerships

This is co-ownership of a business by between two and twenty people; typically four or five. Partners have equal responsibilities and share profits and losses. This form of business is often found in professions such as accountancy, dentistry, law and estate agencies.

Advantages

- Simple to establish as a formal agreement is not necessary, although it is highly desirable in order to agree on conditions and areas of responsibility to avoid any future problems.

- Provides access to more finance.
- Spreads workload and allows for specialists in particular areas.
- Continuity of business is assured; if one partner leaves, the business still goes on.

Disadvantages

- All partners have unlimited liability for the debts of the business.
- The business does not have a separate legal identity.
- There can be conflict between partners and decision-making can be slow compared with the sole trader model.

Limited Companies

A company is a form of business that has been 'incorporated', i.e. registered with the Registrar of Companies. A company has an existence of its own, a legal identity, separate from its owners.

Under The Companies Act (2006) there must be at least one shareholder and shares can only be sold privately; they are not available to the general public. Mainly small family businesses take this form and it's ideal for start-up enterprises.

Advantages

- Limited liability to the amount of investment put into the company, unless personal guarantees are given.
- Shareholders easily added to the organisation. However, agreement required from existing shareholders first.
- Status/image.
- Separate legal identity.
- Possible advantages on saving tax if profits are high.
- Continuity of existence.

Disadvantages

- Registration required including Memorandum of Association and Articles of Association.
- Filing of audited accounts depending on size of the business.

Co-operatives

This is a form of business organisation where a group of people operate a business collectively. Each member has an equal vote in running the affairs of the business. Profits are shared in proportion to work. Usually registered as an industrial and provident society or company limited by guarantee. The minimum number of members is two. Often set up by a group of redundant workers with similar skills. John Lewis is an example of co-operative organisation.

Advantages

- Democratic control of the enterprise by workers and members.
- Model rules for ease of registration.
- Shares easily re-purchased by society when a member leaves.
- Organised for the benefit of members who work in the business.
- Members share in profits.
- Simpler rules and reporting requirements than companies.

Disadvantages

- Management can be hampered by democratic procedures and, therefore, slow to react to changes.
- Investments pay only a fixed rate of interest (unlike shares) and cannot be bought or sold.
- Difficult to attract outside risk capital.
- Need to file audited accounts.
- Cost of registration.

Franchises

Franchising is a form of business in which a product or service may be provided by people or firms who have obtained a licence from the owners of that product or service. Usually it is a well-developed and reputable product or service, well known to the public, e.g. The Body Shop, Kentucky Fried Chicken, McDonalds and many others.

The franchisor (originator) provides a complete package for marketing the product including the name and logo, patented processes, marketing strategy, training and often national advertising. The franchisee has to pay for this package, find suitable premises and equip them to the franchisor's house-style, buy equipment and market the product to specified standards.

Advantages

- Ensures product has been thoroughly tested and marketed.
- Provides a well-known brand name and image and large scale advertising backup.
- Limits the risk of setting up in business.
- Requires less capital than some other forms of business start-up.
- Parent company provides continuing backup support.
- Franchisee may be able to take advantage of economies of scale provided by large organisation, e.g. bulk buying and stock/materials.

Disadvantages

- Cost of some packages is high.
- Franchisee may resent degree of control exercised by the franchisor.
- Support provided by franchisor is sometimes inadequate.
- Franchise packages need to be studied carefully - some can be highly priced and offer little to the franchisee.
- It is usual for a continuing fee to be paid to the franchisor throughout the period of the franchise, a fixed percentage of weekly takings (typically 3-10 percent).

Public Limited Company

A company may decide to 'go public' when it has grown sufficiently to require more capital and offers its shares for sale, usually on the Stock Exchange. Three conditions must be satisfied in order for a company to be registered as a public company.

It must be:

1. limited by shares and have a share capital,
2. able to meet minimum specified capital requirements,
3. described as a plc. in its articles of association.

Advantages

- Separate legal identity, with rights in law.
- Finance is more easily obtainable than in a private company, from

large and small investors.

- A wider spread of capital supports the continuity of the company.

Disadvantages

- The requirement by the Registrar of Companies to publish trading accounts for inspection.
- Legal formalities in setting up.
- Divorce between ownership and management may become a problem.
- Susceptibility to take-overs by changes in share ownership.

You are required to describe what the business will involve and what form it will take. For example, sole trader, partnership or limited company. Justify your choice of business model.

The following diagram can also assist you with your decision as to what type of business model you should adopt if you are going to be a small start-up enterprise.

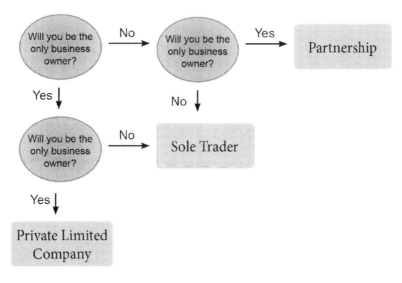

Business models can change over time. The case study below is an example of a situation where the model was changed to minimise risk. I have many years of experience in advising business owners on the type of business model to adopt. Whichever model is adopted, it should minimise the risks and allow you to gain financial freedom efficiently.

CASE STUDY EXAMPLE – FLOORS DIRECT (www.floorsdirectltd.co.uk)

After graduating with a degree in Business Management, the owner wanted to put the theory that he had learnt on the course into practice by setting up in business. Also, times were tough and there weren't many graduate jobs about. However, due to limited resources the owner felt it would be wise to start a small-scale operation.

The business supplies flooring solutions to the general public. Initially, a container load of laminated flooring products was purchased from overseas to test the market. The owner set up as a sole trader business within three months of trading by registering his enterprise with the tax authorities with our assistance at AMCI office. Feedback was positive from the marketplace, they placed more orders overseas and the business got off the ground.

With advice on business planning and development from me and the owner's determination and hard work, the business was finally incorporated into a private limited company after the first year of trading. The main reason for incorporation was to minimise the risks of trading for a growing business and to protect the owner's personal assets as the company has a limited liability. Also, it was tax efficient to do so compared with the sole trader business model.

Business growth has been such that the company has become one of the largest nationwide flooring suppliers dedicated to delivering high quality, reliable and affordable cheap flooring solutions to the general public. Over the years, the investment of a carefully crafted business plan has therefore led to a great deal of success and continues to do so.

Mission Statement and Objectives

This section should give a clear idea of what you are in business for.

Mission Statement

Many businesses have a brief mission statement, usually in thirty words or less, explaining their reason for being and their guiding core values. Mission statements should surprise, delight, inspire and transform to provide purpose and help unify organisations. They go hand-in-hand with the corporate culture. They also help guide a business's inbound marketing content strategy and business blogging.

When a business successfully creates a connection with their customers, suppliers and employees, many of them might stay loyal for life. This helps increase overall profitability while building a solid foundation of brand promoters.

But achieving that connection is no easy task. The businesses that succeed are the ones that stay true to their core values over the years and create a company that employees and customers are proud to associate with.

Here are some examples of mission statements:

- *Honest Tea:* To create and promote great-tasting, healthy, organic beverages.

- *Google:* Google's mission is to organize the world's information and make it universally accessible and useful.

- *Ikea:* At IKEA our vision is to create a better everyday life for the many people. Our business idea supports this vision by offering a wide range of well-designed, functional home furnishing products at prices so low that as many people as possible will be able to afford them.

- *AMCI:* Our mission is to add value to our small and medium-sized clients' business and financial development. Our talented people are passionate in providing unparalleled service to delight our clientele so that they can achieve their goals, profitably.

Core Values

There are normally three or four core values to your business model and service philosophy which you believe will enable your business to stand out and succeed, such as strategic alliances with partners, commitment to customer satisfaction, etc. It may also help with recruiting top talent as many people are drawn to businesses who share their values.

Here is an example of core values at AMCI, which formed the basis for our company name.

- ATTITUDE

We have the professional competences and adopt a positive attitude in solving your problems, however big or small they might be. For example, if you are undergoing a tax investigation by HMRC, contact us so that we can resolve it amicably. We will communicate with you in plain English and undertake an in-depth examination of the situation so that we can clearly understand the nature of the investigation and assist you appropriately in dealing with HMRC.

- MOTIVATION

Our team is highly motivated to make a difference to your bottom line. For example, if you are seeking to raise finance for your new or existing business venture, contact us so that we can assist you to evaluate your proposal to achieve a favourable outcome. We have direct links with high-street banks and other lenders making it easier for you to raise finance!

- CHANGE

From time to time, we all need to adapt to the changing environment. We embrace change as an opportunity for continuous improvement. For example, our advisory services can implement creative and innovative solutions to whatever challenges you might be facing now or in the future. We promise not to let you down!

- INTEGRITY

We take pride in everything that is fair, honest and knowledgeable and build trust in every situation. As your trusted advisors, we are committed to excellence in achieving agreed outcomes. We lead where others follow. Your success is our success!

If you want to draft a mission statement, this is a good place to put it in the plan, followed by:

Company Goals and Objectives

Goals are destinations—where you want your business to be. As such, objectives are progress markers along the road to goal achievement. For example, a goal might be to have a healthy, successful company that is a leader in customer service and that has a loyal customer following. Objectives might be annual sales targets and some specific measures of customer satisfaction.

Objectives should be SMART:

- Specific – related to a specific area such as turnover (sales).
- Measurable – have some means of tracking success, e.g. sales of £1,150,000 in the first year.

- Achievable – based on market research and trends in the industry—your analysis should justify this.

- Realistic – most businesses struggle to make a profit in the first year and so your plan should reflect the expected reality. Also, you need time off, working seven days a week is unrealistic and unsustainable.

- Timely – measured against time, usually a twelve-month period.

State briefly what objectives you are trying to achieve in, say, the first year, two to three years and then three years plus.

Business Concept Outline

- What is your business concept?
- What type of business is it?
- Briefly, what is the need for your business?
- What is your Mission Statement?
- What are your key objectives?

It's time for you to do some work here. The above template can be adapted to complete the Business Concept section. This is also downloadable from www.amci-associates.co.uk/succeed/

SUCCEED!

SECTION 4.   THE KEY PEOPLE

'I've learned that people will forget what you said, people will forget what you did, but people will never forget how you made them feel.'
Maya Angelou – American Poet and Civil Rights Activist

These are the people that will make your enterprise tick. Initially, you might be the only person involved in running your business and therefore have to wear 'several hats'. However, as the business grows, you will need to hire key members of staff and decide what role each of them will take.

Typically, in a value driven business you need to cover the following roles:

Managing Director

This is the leadership position with overall financial responsibility for the success of the business. They will deal with internal and external stakeholders and provide vision, mission and goals for the enterprise.

Quality Controller

This is a key role particularly in food businesses such as restaurants, catering and food processing enterprises. They will ensure agreed quality processes and procedures are always adopted and compliant with legislation and safety standards.

Accountant

This is another key function ensuring the business does not run out of cash and remains profitable. The AMCI business approach offers our clients a specialised service, akin to outsourcing their finance department with significant cost savings!

Receptionist

This person is on the front line. They will be responsible for greeting visitors, handling calls, taking care of the post and other duties assigned by the General Manager.

General Manager

The person in charge of the office and/or shop floor. May be responsible for human resources, marketing and logistics, purchasing and general office/shop floor duties. Once the business has reached a certain size, further specialists can be recruited.

Provide the following information for each person in the form of a CV for inclusion in the appendices to the business plan. An example of a typical CV can be found in the Appendix.

Positions to Be Held within the Organisation

What position will everyone hold in your organisation (e.g. partner, director, etc.)? Define the role and define the skills needed to perform that role. This is a called a job specification and will help you to recruit the people with the right skills and qualifications. People coming into the organisation can be assessed against that criteria and a skills gap matrix created. Understand what they need to learn to be great at that role and put training and experiential opportunities for them to cover their skills gap. This approach improves competency and also creates confidence within the incoming person that they are being supported. Successful organisations see all people as key to the business. If they aren't key, why are they there?

What positions are vacant within the organisation and how, when or do you plan to fill these?

Finance

The following are particularly applicable if you are applying for finance: any finance, assets, property, pension schemes, funds, etc, available to fund the business and who holds this finance. Where does any liability sit? Who owns the asset?

Skills Needed

State whether you have the necessary skills for this business venture and if you are or will be receiving training. Whether you are receiving training or not, can you get a mentor to support you and challenge how you are operating? An alternative to learning the skills yourself is to outsource to others. The job specification can be very useful as a guide to ensuring you are hiring the right level of subcontract skill. When using subcontract labour you may need to consider IR35 and other direct tax deduction requirements for regular workers. Work that is outsourced still needs to be to the correct standard and legal agreements in place to ensure you are not paying for a quality of work that you do not receive.

Key People Outline

- Key people and their roles in your business.
- Positions to be held within your business.
- Finance and funds held to fund the business.
- Skills held.

You can now complete the Key People section by using the above outline. This is also downloadable from www.amci-associates.co.uk/succeed/

SUCCEED!

SECTION 5.   MARKET RESEARCH

'Whoever understands the customer best, wins.'
Mike Gospe – Author of Marketing Campaign Development

Market Research - Why?

No matter how good your product and your service, the venture cannot succeed without effective marketing. Market research begins with careful, systematic research. It is very dangerous to assume that you already know about your intended market. You need to do market research to make sure you're on track. Use the business planning process as your opportunity to uncover data and to question your marketing efforts. Your time will be well spent.

The function of Market Research is to determine the nature and extent of demand, which exists for a product or service. It is necessary to establish what the customer wants and needs in order to provide it.

Businesses need to know:

- What the customer wishes to buy.
- Where he or she prefers to buy it.
- In what quantity and when.

The right product can then be produced to meet this demand.

Market Research - How?

Market research is essential for Sales Forecasting and Planning. Some of the questions to be answered are listed below.

What is the size of the total market?	How many potential customers?
Is the market growing, static or declining?	
What fraction of the market do you hope to obtain?	How many real customers?

Who are your customers?	Lifestyle, age, sex, location, social group, etc.
Who does the buying?	E.g. children create demand for toys but parents pay.
Where is the buying done?	Chain store, mail order, corner shop, etc.
Where are the customers located?	Region of the county, size of town, and local areas.
What kind of product/service do they want?	Price, quality, performance, image, etc.
Why do they want the product?	Basic need, status, fashion.
When do they buy?	How often, how much, seasonal influence.
Who else supplies this product/service?	Competitors - where located, prices, quality, etc.

There are two kinds of market research: primary and secondary.

Primary Research means gathering your own data. For example, you could do your own traffic count at a proposed location, carry out surveys (online using Survey Monkey - www.surveymonkey.co.uk) or focus group interviews to learn about consumer preferences. Professional market research can be very costly, but a lot of this you can do yourself. See Appendix on designing your own questionnaire.

In your marketing plan, be as specific as possible. Give statistics, numbers, and the sources of this information and data to add credibility. The marketing plan will be the basis, later on, of the all-important sales projection.

Secondary Research means using published information such as industry profiles, trade journals, newspapers, magazines, census data, and demographic profiles. This type of information is available from online sources, public libraries, industry associations, chambers of commerce, from vendors who sell to your industry and from government agencies.

Client or End User?

To whom are you hoping to sell your products/service? Consumers can be put into segments (typical customer characteristics) based on location, lifestyle, and demographics. Another way to segment consumers is by asking who, what, and why questions.

You should have a very clear idea of the characteristics of your market segments you are aiming your service or product at. Segments may be identified by one or more of the following:

- The age group(s).
- Gender.
- Socio-economic characteristics.
- Income.
- Level of education.
- Religion.
- Geographical domain of potential customers.
- Other distinguishing characteristics.

Segmentation and targeting segmentation and targeting, influences an organisation's strategy for pricing, communication and customer management.

What pricing structure are you aiming for (e.g. high price/high quality luxury goods such as, Rolex watches, Rolls Royce cars, Waitrose and haute couture clothing, or lower price/lower quality clothing such as Primark clothing, Aldi or Lidl shopping experience)? Try to explain why the market segments you are targeting might try your products or service.

Market research is often the weakest aspect of any application for finance and consequently one that is looked at very carefully by lenders.

There are many areas to consider including:

- Who will be my customers?
- Where will I find them?
- What do they want in terms of quality, price, choice, etc.?
- Where do they prefer to buy?
- Is the business seasonal?

Researching the Target Market Segments

In testing prospective customer opinions/reactions using questionnaires or personal interviews, you will need to discover what groups of people are likely to buy your products or services. Therefore you need to find out:

- What they have done in the past?
- What price they are likely to pay?

- How often they are likely to buy?
- Age, social economic group if relevant.
- Where they are likely to buy?

You also need to consider external influences, which could impact upon your target markets in the future, by considering what is known as the 'remote environment'.

The Remote Environment

The remote environment comprises factors that originate beyond, and are usually irrespective of, any single organisation's operating situation and can include the following factors:

- Political.
- Economic.
- Social.
- Technological.
- Ecological.

Although these factors affect your organisation's decision-making freedom and abilities and are beyond your influence or control, these environmental factors present opportunities, threats, and constraints, but rarely does a single firm exert any meaningful reciprocal influence. For example, when the economy slows and construction starts to decrease, an individual contractor is likely to suffer a decline in business, but that contractor's efforts in stimulating local construction activities would be unable to reverse the overall decrease in construction.

Economics - Facts about Your Industry

- What is the total size of your market?
- What percent share of the market will you have? (This is important only if you think you will be a major factor in the market.)
- Current demand in the target market.
- Trends in the target market - growth trends, trends in consumer preferences and trends in product development.
- Growth potential and opportunities for a business of your size.

What barriers to entry do you face in entering this market with your new company? Some typical barriers are:

- High capital costs (e.g. airlines, venues, hotels).
- High production costs (e.g. car factories, other engineering firms).
- High marketing costs (e.g. telecom service providers, luxury goods such BMW 7 series).
- Consumer acceptance and brand recognition (e.g. Samsung devices, Apple iPhones).
- Training and skills (e.g. mechanical, civil and structural engineers).
- Unique technology and patents (e.g. Apple, Samsung).
- Unions (Unisons, CBI).
- Shipping costs (exports/imports especially in light of Brexit).
- Tariff barriers and quotas (in light of Brexit).

And of course, how will you overcome the barriers?

How could the following affect your company?

- Changes in technology.
- Changes in government regulations.
- Changes in the economy.
- Changes in society.
- Changes in your industry.

Competitor Analysis

What products and companies will compete with you?

List your major competitors:

- Names, addresses and websites.
- Will they compete with you across the board, or just for certain products, certain customers, or in certain locations?
- Will you have important indirect competitors? (For example, Netflix compete with theatres, although they are different types of businesses.)
- How will your products or services compare with the competition?

I have produced a Competitive Analysis table on the next page that will assist you in comparing your company with your most important competitors. In the first column are key competitive factors. Since these vary from one industry to another, you may want to customise the list of factors.

In the column labeled Me, state how you honestly think you will stack up in customers' minds giving scores of 1 to 5 (1 being critical whereas 5 not very important). Then check whether you think this factor will be a strength or a weakness for you (tick either the strength or weakness column). Sometimes it is hard to analyse our own weaknesses. Try to be objective here. Better yet, get a neutral party to assess you—this can be a real eye-opener. Remember that you cannot be all things to all people. In fact, trying to be causes many business failures, because efforts become scattered and diluted. You want an honest assessment of your firm's strong and weak points. Similarly, give scores of 1 to 5 for your key competitors. This will then allow you to determine the importance of these factors to your customers using the scale of 1 to 5. Make sure you concentrate on 1s and 2s as these are critical to your success.

Now analyse each major competitor. In a few words, state how you think they compare.

FACTOR	Me	Strength	Weakness	Competitor A	Competitor B	Importance to Customer
Products						
Price						
Quality						
Selection						
Service						
Reliability						
Stability						
Expertise						
Company Reputation						
Location						
Appearance						
Sales Method						
Credit Policies						
Advertising						
Image						

Results of Market Research

- You must demonstrate a clear understanding of who your prospective customers are, how many there are, how much will they spend and when will they buy.

- If you have produced a questionnaire this should be included in the Business Plan as an appendix.

- You must then be able to show how these market research findings back up your projected sales figures.

Market Research Outline

- Your targeted market segments.

- Who will be my customers, where will I find them, what do they want in terms of quality, price, choice, etc, and where do they prefer to buy from?

- Market research.

- What have customers done in the past; what price they are likely to pay and how often and where are they likely to buy? Consider age and social economic groups if relevant.

- Factors in the remote environment likely to influence demand?

- Competitor analysis (key points).

-

You can now complete the Market Research section by using this template. This is also downloadable from www.amci-associates.co.uk/succeed/

SECTION 6. MARKETING PLAN AND STRATEGY

'You have to understand your target customer and what you're trying to sell them.'
Daniel McGaw – Founder of Effin Amazing

Decide what market you are really in. Are you selling Toyotas or Ferraris?

Marketing strategy then follows. Two key factors here are price and quality. The following diagram sums up the relationship well:

<table>
<tr><td rowspan="2"></td><td rowspan="2"></td><td colspan="3">QUALITY</td></tr>
<tr><td>Low</td><td>Medium</td><td>High</td></tr>
<tr><td rowspan="3">PRICES</td><td>Low</td><td>Cheap high volume</td><td>Bargain price</td><td>Giveaway</td></tr>
<tr><td>Medium</td><td>Shoddy goods</td><td>Middle of the road</td><td>Penetration/ under pricing</td></tr>
<tr><td>High</td><td>Hit and run</td><td>Overpricing</td><td>Luxury goods</td></tr>
</table>

Assessment of strengths and weaknesses versus competition is important here.

Product Strategy

Product strategy is concerned with various aspects of the product or service.

Quality/performance	Is the product technically sound? Is it the quality demanded by customers?
Identity	Is there a distinctive name or trademark?
Features/options	Does the product have all the features required by customers? Is the service flexible enough to offer options?
Design/style	This concerns the look of the product and smooth efficiency of service.

Packaging	Does it do the job it is intended to? Is it in line with the product?
Warranty	Is there provision for after sales service or guarantees?
Availability	Can the customer easily obtain/find the product?

Pricing Strategy

Pricing strategy is a vital aspect of marketing and a product's success or failure may depend upon the value placed upon it in the market place.

Level	Is the price level right for customers in the target market segment?
Discounts	Is the price right for your company?
Changes	How does your price compare with competitors' prices? What image of product does the price project?
Payment terms	High price, high quality, value for money, cheap and cheerful, bargain, etc.

Promotion

Promotional strategy is based on communication between the firm and the consumer in order to inform and then persuade the customer to buy its products. It combines one or more of the following:

Advertising	Newspapers Magazines TV and radio Billboards Social media: Facebook, Instagram, Google ads, etc.
Personal selling	Face to face in company, shop, etc. Telephone
Direct mail	Mail shots Leaflet distribution

Product literature	Company literature Instructions Brochures, etc.
Exhibitions	National, local
Shop window	Point of sale display signs
Sponsorships	Sporting events, etc.
Sales promotion	Special offers, etc.

Advertising

Advertising is a technique by which products and services are brought to the notice of prospective purchasers using various media. The main purposes of advertising is to inform and persuade.

Format of Advertising

A -	Attention	must be eye-catching
I -	Interest	mention major features
D -	Desire	match features to benefits for customer
A -	Action	give enough information to help customer find your product easily

Personal Selling

This is the person-to-person approach between a member of a company's sales force and a potential customer.

Sales staff often supply technical details and other information regarding special offers, discounts, new products, etc.

Direct Mail

This can be a good way of getting product information to specific groups of potential customers. It can be used to target a large number of people with up-to-date details of special offers or seasonal promotions. A response mechanism is usually included. Please make sure that you are compliant with GDPR regulations.

Product Literature

Brochures and leaflets can be used to send out in response to sales queries or as part of a mail shot. A brochure should describe the product, highlight the benefits and reflect the style or image of the business. Leaflets are cheaper than brochures and often contain details of a special event or offer.

Exhibitions

Trade exhibitions are another form of direct selling and promotion. They are also sources of information on competitors.

Shop Windows

Displays and point of sale literature need to be eye catching in order to promote impulse buying.

Sponsorships

This method of promoting a business name or company image is becoming increasingly popular. Many sponsorships involve sporting events and participants but other areas are now attracting sponsors including music and other arts.

Sales Promotion

Other activities, which support advertising campaigns, are referred to as sales promotion and include the following:

- Special offers: e.g. twin packs, extra value, money off, etc.
- Coupons: redeemable against cost of product.
- Samples: small samples of product, trial packs.
- Giveaways: pencils, pens, funny hats, etc.

Digital Tracking

There are many online platforms where your products can be promoted and seen by a targeted market. Using the algorithms created by platforms such as Facebook can increase visibility of your product or service and provide a sales portal. Tracking can be put in place across social media to understand the habits of your potential customers and to ensure when they are on social media they see you.

Distribution Strategy

Distribution refers to the means by which goods and services get from producers to consumers. It is vital that customers have access to the product when and where they want it.

The means of distribution are constantly changing in order to suit:

- Changing products.
- Market changes.
- Customer needs and preferences.

The three main forms of distribution are:

- Direct selling.
- Retailing.
- Wholesaling.

Direct Selling

This is a technique whereby the producer supplies the consumer directly without using a retailer. A boost to this type of selling has been the increasing popularity of payment by credit cards.

Direct selling can take several forms:

- Door-to-door selling - e.g. double glazing and other home improvements.
- Advertisements in newspapers and magazines.
- TV and radio advertisements.
- Telephone sales using a Freephone service.
- Mail shots using Freepost and Business Reply Service.
- Party plan selling - party organiser arranges delivery.
- Vending machines - airports, stations and workplaces.
- Service industries - from hotels to plumbers, providing service directly to customers.

Wholesaling

Traditionally the wholesaler provides the link between producers and retailers. There is an increasing tendency for producers to bypass the wholesaler and sell directly to the public and for large retailers to bulk buy directly from producers.

The main function of wholesalers is to buy in bulk from producers and then resell in smaller amounts to retailers. This serves a very useful purpose to small shops and businesses that stock many different lines and who have neither the storage capacity or purchasing power for bulk buying.

Retailing

Retailers form the final link in the chain between producers and consumers.

Retailers deal directly with customers and, therefore, changing customer needs and tastes have brought about changes in retailing, e.g. the emergence of out of town hypermarkets and shopping centres with refreshment and play areas that fulfill the role of a leisure activity for consumers.

Forms of Retailing

- The small independent shop, e.g. corner shop.
- Department stores - many departments within one store.
- Chain stores - with several branches that can be specialist or variable.
- Supermarkets/hypermarkets.
- Mail order - recently enjoying renewed interest with new entrants to market. Also specialist mail order, e.g. book clubs.

Target Market

Who is the target market?

Fully explain your marketing strategy including the 5Ws and 1H:

- What is your product or service?
- Who is it aimed at?
- When you will offer it?
- Where you will offer it?
- Why do you think there is a market for it?
- How will you offer it?

Targeting Customers

Identify your targeted customers, their characteristics, and their geographic locations, otherwise known as their demographics.

The description will be completely different depending on whether you plan to sell to other businesses (B2B: wholesalers, business and professional services) or directly to consumers (B2C: retailers, most gyms). If you sell a consumer product, but sell it through a channel of distributors, wholesalers, and retailers, you must carefully analyse both the end consumer and the middleman businesses to which you sell.

You may have more than one customer group. Identify the most important groups. Then, for each customer group, construct what is called a demographic profile:

- Age.
- Gender.
- Location.
- Income level.
- Social class and occupation.
- Education.
- Other (specific to your industry).

For business customers, the demographic factors might be:

- Industry (or portion of an industry).
- Location (physical, online, etc.).
- Size of firm.
- Quality, technology, and price preferences.

Marketing Planning

'In life, as in football, you won't go far unless you know where the goalposts are.'
Arnold H Glasgow – Entrepreneur

Traditional marketing is a combination of the 4 Ps:

- Price.
- Product.

- Place.
- Promotion.

But in service sectors there are an additional 3 Ps to consider:

- Process.
- Physical ambience (atmosphere).
- People – the employees (or yourself) who deliver the service.

Pricing

Explain your method or methods of setting prices. For most small businesses, having the lowest price is not necessarily a good policy. It robs you of needed profit margin; customers may not care as much about price as you think and large competitors can under price you anyway. Usually you will do better to have average prices and compete on quality and service.

Does your pricing strategy fit with what was revealed in your competitive analysis?

- Are your competitors market leaders?
- Do they regularly compete on price?
- Can you compete with their marketing strategies?

How important is price as a competitive factor? Do your intended customers really make their purchase decisions mostly on price?

What will be your customer service and credit policies?

Calculation of Selling Price

Points to consider:

- Will you be selling a high quality product/service at a high price or a lower quality at a lower price?
- What profit margin do you require?
- Does cost of production plus required profit give you a realistic selling price? Compare to market research findings on prices.
- How do your prices compare with those of competitors? If higher can costs be reduced to give a more competitive price?
- Costs?

Cost is something that can be classified in several ways depending on its nature. The usual method is a classification according to fixed costs and variable costs. Fixed costs do not change with increases/decreases in units of production/service volume (interest on loans or business rates bills on premises), while variable costs are solely dependent on the volume of units of production/service (such as the costs associated with energy and raw materials).

Show how you have calculated your costs and give examples. Here is a worked example to assist you.

Worked Example - Capital Tours Ltd

Capital Tours Ltd. is organising a theatre break package to London, which will consist of a night's stay at a hotel with evening meal and breakfast and a theatre ticket for a popular show.

The following costs, excluding VAT, of organising this theatre break have been estimated as follows:

Cost per show ticket	£22.00
Accommodation costs per person	£30.00
Food and beverage costs per person	£15.00

Other costs, including VAT, of the package will be coach hire £360, advertising and marketing costs at £420, and labour and administration charges, excluding VAT, at £220. VAT is charged at 20%.

The coach will hold 90 paying passengers.

Calculate a selling price, including VAT, to make a 25% profit margin for the Capital Tours Ltd.

Net profit Pricing:

(a) Determine variable costs per person

Cost per show ticket	£22
Food and beverage costs	£15
Accommodation costs	£30
Total variable cost per person	£67

(b) Determine fixed costs

Coach hire (£360 x 100/120)	£300
Advertising and marketing (£420 x 100/120)	£350
Labour costs	£220
Total fixed costs	£870

Total costs:

Variable (£67 x 90 people)	£6030
Fixed costs (see above)	£870
	£6900

i)   Cost per person will be £76.67 (£6900/90 people)
i)   Net profit target required is 25%

Therefore, selling price will be £102.23 (£76.67 x 100/(100 - 25))

Selling price including VAT will be £122.68 (£102.23 x 120/100)

Possibly round it to £123.

Activity 1: Calculate selling price if 20% net profit margin is required by Capital Tours Ltd.

Activity 2: Calculate selling price if 7% net profit margin is required by Capital Tours Ltd.

Solutions to Activity 1:

Ex VAT: £95.84 ((£76.67 x 100/(100 - 20))

VAT inclusive (price paid by the customer): £115.00 (£95.84 x 120/100)

Solutions to Activity 2:

Ex VAT: £82.44 ((£76.67 x 100/(100 - 7))

VAT inclusive (price paid by the customer): £98.93 (£82.44 x 120/100)
Possibly round it to £99

Do You Know Your Break-Even Point and How Long Will It Take to Reach This?

The break-even point is reached when the number of units of a product or service sold provides enough sales revenue to cover the total costs involved in their production/service, both fixed and variable. The break-even point represents the minimum number of units that must be sold to cover costs. At this point no profit is made.

Cost of Materials/Stock (Per Month)

Stock/raw materials needed each month obviously relates directly to sales; the more you sell the more materials/stock you require.

The amount of stock/raw materials can be calculated as a percentage of resulting sales value and this enables you to easily estimate stock requirements for all levels of sales. If several different materials/components are used, give details. Will increased purchases of stock/materials attract better discounts? Will it be possible to obtain stock as you need it to avoid having working capital tied up in stock?

Also, do not forget the value of your time. If you calculate that you are going to offer a service at £23/hr but may only have six clients in 10hrs, your actual hourly rate is £13.80 (£23 x 6/10).

Remember that you need time off. No business (without other staff) can operate seven days a week. Take care of your health too.

Looking back at the Capital Tours Ltd. example, let's calculate the break-even point assuming that they have gone with a 7% net profit margin.

Here we need to work with VAT exclusive figures.

Break-even point = Fixed costs
                   Contribution per unit

Contribution per unit = Selling price – variable costs

Calculate the contribution per unit first, which in the case of Capital Tours Ltd. is as follows:

£98.93 - £76.67 = £22.26

Break-even point = £870 = 39.1 customers.
                   £22.26

Therefore, Capital Tours Ltd. need 40 customers to break-even or in other words, cover all the costs of the tour!

In other words, if they have full capacity of 90 paying passengers, the tour will be highly profitable.

Total profit being sales minus cost:

Sales (£98.93 x 90)		£8904
Less costs:	Variable cost (£76.67 x 90)	£6900
Fixed cost		£ 870
Total costs		£7770
NET PROFIT PER TOUR		£1134

Activity 3: Calculate the break-even point and total net profit if a 25% net profit margin is required.

Activity 4: Calculate the break-even point and total net profit if a 20% net profit margin is required.

Solutions to Activity 3:

Calculate the break-even point and total net profit if a 25% net profit margin is required.

Break-even point = Fixed costs
                   Contribution per unit

Contribution per unit is: Selling price – variable costs

Calculate the contribution per unit first, which in the case of Capital Tours Ltd. is as follows:

£102.23 - £76.67 = £25.56

Break-even point = £870 = 34 customers.
                    £25.56

Total profit being sales minus cost:

Sales (£102.23 x 90)	£9201
Less costs: Variable cost (£76.67 x 90)	£6900
Fixed cost	£ 870
Total costs	£7770
NET PROFIT PER TOUR	£1431

Solutions to Activity 4:

Calculate the break- even point and total net profit if a 20% net profit margin is required.

Break-even point = Fixed costs
                   Contribution per unit

Contribution per unit is: Selling price – variable costs

Calculate the contribution per unit first, which in the case of Capital

Tours Ltd. is as follows:

£95.84 - £76.67 = £19.17

Break-even point = $\frac{£870}{£19.17}$ = 45.4.customers.

Therefore, Capital Tours Ltd. needs 46 customers to break-even or in other words, cover all the costs of the tour!

Total profit being sales minus cost

Sales (£95.84 x 90)	£8626
Less costs: Variable cost (£76.67 x 90)	£6900
Fixed cost	£ 870
Total costs	£7770
NET PROFIT PER TOUR	£ 856

Cost Plus

This is a popular method of pricing—the easiest way is to calculate your costs and add on the percentage of profit you want to make per transaction.

For example if your costs per item/service are £20 and you want to make 50% profit, your selling price would be £30 (£20 x 150/100). Using this method, you need to remember your costs and then you can discount your selling price to attract new customers, be that through promotions or if targeting corporate/wholesale customers. Capital Tours Ltd. is a worked example of cost plus pricing, also known as net profit pricing.

Price discounting can be managed effectively through a technique called 'marginal pricing'. Marginal pricing is a method used particularly for short-term decisions. The majority of decisions faced by you involve a choice between alternative courses of action, strategies or policies. In making such decisions, considerable importance needs to be attached to the identification of those costs that are relevant to the particular course of action under consideration.

Price Discounting Example: Capital Tours Ltd.

In the case of the Capital Tours Ltd. example, the selling price inclusive of

VAT for the theatre break package was calculated at £122.68 (£102.23 x 120/100). However, we need to use selling price exclusive of VAT and that was £102.23 per person.

A week before the theatre break is due to take place there are still twenty-five unsold places. A person contacts Capital Tours Ltd. through its website and offers to pay £80 excluding VAT for the theatre break package. Should this offer be accepted on financial grounds?

Marginal Pricing decisions are based upon assessing the 'contribution' being earned from a product or service.

> ## Contribution = Selling Price less Marginal Costs

Contribution is a measure of the financial benefit that the sale of a product gives to a business in order to help it cover its fixed costs and to make profits. The theory is that in the short-term, provided a discounted price is covering the variable costs and contributing something towards fixed costs then it is a mistake to reject it, unless there is an alternative which gives a greater contribution to put in its place.

In the long-term, services must be priced to cover variable costs, fixed costs and to make a profit and consequently a marginal pricing approach to calculations is generally only applicable in restricted circumstances. An obvious example here would be when a company has sold some but not all the tickets near to the departure date of a tour but is committed to the tour going ahead.

In the case of Capital Tours Ltd. the contribution per person was calculated at:

£102.23 - £76.67 = £25.56

Based on this scenario, the price of £80 per person should be accepted as it is above £76.67 (the marginal cost). Each person in the discounted category therefore makes a contribution of:

£80.00 - £76.67 = £3.33

The total contribution towards overall profitability will be:

£3.33 x 25 customers = £83.25.

Activity 5: What if the discounted price offered was £80 inclusive of VAT. Should the price be accepted?

Solution to Activity 5:

You need to eliminate VAT from the price before calculating contribution.

£80 x 100/120 = £66.67 per person

Contribution = Selling Price less Marginal Costs

£66.67 - £76.67 = (£10.00) implying Capital Tours Ltd. would be making a loss!

Since the contribution is negative, Capital Tours Ltd. should reject the offer as this would cost the company £10 per person each time this price is accepted!

Once you are happy working through the examples above, use your own prices and costs to check your profitability.

Product

Describe in depth your products or services (technical specifications, drawings, photos, sales brochures, and other bulky items belong in Appendices).

Features and Benefits

For each product or service:

- Describe the most important features. What is special about it?
- Describe the benefits. That is, what will the product do for the customer?

Note the difference between features and benefits, and think about them carefully. For example, a house that gives shelter and lasts a long time is made with certain materials and to a certain design, which are its features. Its benefits include pride of ownership, financial security, providing for the family, and inclusion in a neighbourhood. You need to build similar features into your product so that you can sell the benefits.

Now describe them from your customers' point of view. What are your customers buying?

What after-sale services will you give? Some examples are delivery, warranty, service contracts, support, follow-up, and refund policy.

What factors will give you competitive advantages or disadvantages? Examples include level of quality or unique or proprietary features. Competitive advantage is what makes your business stand out from the competition. True competitive advantage is rarely gained through technology as this can be easily copied. Instead it is usually a combination of people and tacit knowledge. That is, knowledge which is particular to your company, such as your customer service procedures, your stock management/distribution procedures or something specific in the service you give.

Place - Proposed Location

Do you have a precise location (physical, online or a combination) picked out yet? This is the time to think about what you want and need in a location. Many business start-ups run successfully from home in the digital age for a while, or do you want to be mobile?

You will need to describe your physical needs (size, cost, etc) later, in the Operational Plan section.

Here, analyse your location criteria as they will affect your customers:

- Is your location important to your customers? If yes, how?

If customers come to your place of business:

- Is it convenient? Parking? Interior spaces? Not out of the way?
- Is it consistent with your image?
- Is it what customers want and expect?
- Where is the competition located? Is it better for you to be near them (like car dealers or fast-food restaurants) or distant (like convenience-food stores)?

Promotion

How will you get the word out to customers?

Advertising: What media, why, and how often? Why this mix and not some other?

Have you identified low-cost methods to get the most out of your promotional budget?

Will you use methods other than paid advertising, such as trade shows, catalogues, dealer incentives, word of mouth (how will you stimulate it?), and network of friends or professionals?

What image do you want to project? How will you position your business, meaning how do you want customers to see you?

In addition to advertising, what plans do you have for graphic image support? This includes things like logo design, cards and letterhead, brochures, signage, and interior design (if customers come to your place of business).

Should you have a system to identify repeat customers and then systematically contact them?

Promotional Budget

How much will you spend on the items listed above? Before start-up? (These numbers will go into your start-up budget.) Ongoing? (These numbers will go into your operating plan budget.)

Distribution Channels

How do you sell your products or services?

- Retail.
- Direct (mail order, web, catalog).
- Wholesale.
- Your own sales force.
- Agents.
- Independent representatives.
- Bid on contracts.

Your Niche

What is your niche? What are your USP (Unique Selling Propositions) which differentiate you from competitors? What strategy will you adopt?

Now that you have systematically analysed your industry, your product, your customers, and the competition, you should have a clear picture of where your company fits into the world.

To assess your competition, look around your immediate industry/sector and then look across sectors as there may be some businesses in other sectors which offer a similar service to you. From a business risk focus, it is important that you are aware of these, even if your risk assessment deems them to be negligible. Nevertheless, these services/companies/sectors might provide you with inspiration for another potential market.

Write a short paragraph which defines your niche, your unique corner of the market.

Marketing Strategy

In this section you should explain how you will market your product/service such as direct selling, etc; how, where and when will you advertise your business, along with any strategic alliances or partnerships you plan to make.

Do not forget to put the costs for this into your finance section and make sure your marketing strategy is consistent with your niche market:

- Emerging market?
- Saturated market?
- Growth or declining market?

Stay out of declining markets if you intend to establish a robust business.

How Will You Stand Out from the Competition?

Is your service/company entering an established market with existing companies or a new market with very few direct competitors? If there are lots of existing businesses you will need to possess something special to stand out—this will need to be something sustainable, beyond a marketing gimmick.

For most small businesses it is not realistic to try to be the 'price leader', i.e. have the lowest prices. There will always be other companies/services which will try to undercut you, and price wars can detract from customer service, prevent long-term growth and seriously cripple a business. A prime example is the low cost airlines, which are constantly competing for market share by slashing their prices and virtually giving away their seats and breaking down their service to the bare minimum.

These companies make their money through add-ons such as inflight meals and drinks, which are standard on other 'full-cost carriers' or passenger changes such as flight times and car hire, hotels, insurance, etc. The companies lose money on the customers who do not change their flight, do not eat or drink onboard (or take their own supplies) and do not require ground services, but they need to do this in order to stay competitive within the 'price/cost leadership' strategy.

New or Saturated Market?

If it is a saturated market you may consider a strategic alliance with direct competitors or ancillary services.

If you are entering a new market you will need to assess the demand for your product/service—your market research should tell you this. But if there is negligible demand, you may need to stimulate demand. This will require a dynamic marketing strategy or a strategic alliance within or across industries.

Growth or Declining Market?

In a growing/expanding market public sentiment, both from financiers and customers, tends to be fairly high and a generic business model will usually suffice to attract money and clients.

In a declining market though or an established (mature) market where innovations are slow, you will need to demonstrate a robust business model to attract external finance and a solid market presence to develop a customer base.

If you get to this stage and you cannot identify a USP about your business or a niche market for it, or a dynamic positioning strategy, you should reconsider the whole venture! If you are unable to see 'the spark of genius' behind the business, as the creator, who is presumably full of passion for the enterprise, then chances are your potential investors will not see it as a viable proposition.

Digital Marketing

The world is undergoing a digital transformation. Therefore, it is important that in the digital age you are able to define, design, build and implement digital campaigns across a variety of online and social media platforms. You need to create a digital presence for your products and services. You should have a website, be visible on Facebook, Instagram, and if you are providing B2B services, make sure to have LinkedIn and Twitter accounts.

I can assist you to find the right consultants to work with you in designing a digital strategy. Contact us for further information (info@amci-associates.co.uk). Digital marketing is a must in the 21st century; ignore it at your own peril!

Projected Sales

Now that you have described your products, services, customers, markets, and marketing plans in detail, it's time to attach some numbers to your plan in order to check that you are on target. Use a sales forecast spreadsheet to prepare a month-by-month projection. Good news, we have created sales forecasting software to assist you here...

Your sales forecast is all about setting goals for your business. You are looking to answer questions such as:

- What do you hope to achieve in the next twelve months, year two and year three?

- How many customers do you hope to have in the next twelve months, year two and year three?

- How much will each customer spend on average with your business?

The forecast should be based on your historical sales, the marketing strategies that you have just described, your market research, and industry data, if available. This is an important section if you are hoping to apply for financial assistance from banks and other finance providers.

It is important to prepare the projected sales (sales forecast) on a month-by-month basis at least for a twelve months period. Year two and year three can consist of annual figures with appropriate uplift based on your research.

Why do you think you can sell this amount at this price?

Projected sales are the estimated sales that you hope to achieve. You may want to do two forecasts:

1) A 'best guess', which is what you really expect, and

2) a 'worst case' low estimate that you are confident you can reach no matter what happens.

It is important to keep notes on your research and your assumptions as you build this sales forecast and all subsequent spreadsheets in the plan. This is critical if you are going to present it to acquire start-up finance.

Can you cope with producing these quantities?

(How much labour is needed, how much advertising to promote sales, will equipment cope?)

Explain seasonal variations of demand if any and how you anticipate sales increasing over the first year. For instance, are you expecting to increase the price or quantities sold or both and why?

CASE STUDY EXAMPLE - SKIRTING WORLD (WWW.MDFSKIRTINGWORLD.CO.UK)

The business was set up by school friends, Marc Greene and Ian Allen. Both of them were working in a factory supplying skirting boards and architraves to the building industry when they were in their early twenties.

Both friends initially undertook market research consisting of desk research (secondary research) to determine the size and growth of the sector. Once this was completed contacts were made with potential customers to determine if they will do business with them. Having completed thorough market research, both friends identified a gap in the market of supplying the skirting boards and architraves directly to the customer.

Competitor analysis was undertaken. Marc and Ian found they could do a better job on their own by producing a range of solutions that was considerably superior and also largely supplying the products directly to the consumer by 'cutting out the middleman'. Further marketing efforts included setting up the website and seeking an advisor (AMCI) who was willing to support their efforts every step of the way.

Customers are able to place orders directly through the website, by

---

telephone or by visiting the factory showroom. Promotion also consists of sponsoring a local boxer, who recently won a European Championship, sponsoring a junior football team, bill boards and adopting an effective social media strategy.

The business is centrally located in the Midlands and therefore able to reach its customers throughout the UK with ease. Also, the business is able to supply bespoke solutions cost effectively. Supplying the products directly to the consumer has led to significant cost saving and a great deal of financial freedom for Marc and Ian. By following a carefully crafted marketing strategy and financial advice supporting a high growth enterprise, the business has not only reported double digit growth year on year in Turnover but also in Operating Profit.

Marketing Plan & Strategy Outline

- Targeting customers
- Market planning – Price
- Market planning – Place
- Market planning – Promotion
- Your niche
- How will you stand out from competitors?
- Sales forecasts (one – three years)

If you wish, you can prepare the sales forecast for your business venture using the FREE sales forecasting software that comes with the book or use the ones I have prepared available to download on the website.

You can complete the Marketing Plan and Strategy section by using the outline above. This is also downloadable from www.amci-associates.co.uk/succeed/

SECTION 7. OPERATIONS

'Isn't it what we repeatedly do? Excellence, then is not an act, but a habit.'
Aristotle – Greek Philosopher

Explain the daily operation of the business, its location, equipment, people, processes and surrounding environment.

Production

How and where are your products or services produced?

Explain your methods of:
- Production techniques and costs.
- Quality control.
- Customer service.
- Inventory control.
- Product development.

Equipment

Identify large items of equipment/machinery, etc. If possible obtain leaflets and brochures.

Obtain prices from several suppliers. Evaluate prices, terms offered and after sales service.

Location

What qualities do you need in a location? Describe the type of location you'll have.

Physical requirements:
- Amount of space.
- Type of building.
- Power and other utilities.

Access:

- Is it important that your location be convenient to transportation or to suppliers? Do you need easy walk-in access? What are your requirements for parking and proximity to airports, trains, and motorways?

- Include a drawing or layout of your proposed facility if it is important, as it might be for a manufacturer.

Costs

- Estimate your occupation expenses such as rent, rates, maintenance, utilities, insurance, and initial remodeling costs to make the space suit your needs. If you need to change the layout, is planning permission required? These numbers will become part of your financial plan.

- What will be your business hours?

- When and how are these costs to be paid? Six months in advance is not uncommon. Are there any other charges, e.g. maintenance fee, insurance or business rates?

- Consider cost and length of lease and cost of necessary legal fees.

- Cost of renovation, redecoration and furnishing of premises.

Legal Environment

Describe the following:

- Technology and specialised equipment requirements.
- Licensing and bonding requirements.
- Professional associations – membership fees.
- Health, workplace, or environmental regulations.
- Special regulations covering your industry or profession.
- Planning permission.
- Insurance coverage – personal and public liability.
- Trademarks, copyrights, or patents (pending, existing, or purchased).
-

Personnel

- Number of employees.
- Type of labour (skilled, unskilled, and professional).

- Where and how will you find the right employees?
- Quality of existing staff.
- Pay structure.
- Training methods and requirements.
- Who does which tasks? Do you have schedules and written procedures prepared?

Have you drafted job descriptions for employees? If not, take time to write some using the template below. They really help with internal communications with employees.

Job Title:	
Salary Range:	
Reports To:	
Job Purpose:	
Main Duties and Responsibilities:	

For certain functions, will you use contract workers in addition to employees?

Inventory

- What kind of inventory will you keep, e.g. raw materials, supplies, finished goods?
- Average value in stock (i.e. what is your inventory investment)?
- Rate of turnover and how this compares to the industry averages?
- Seasonal build-ups, e.g. at Christmas, Easter, Eid, Diwali?
- What is the lead-time for ordering? That is, how much time does it take to receive the goods?

Suppliers

It is necessary to investigate sources of suppliers and find out:

- Names, addresses and websites.
- Prices.
- Minimum order levels.
- What discounts are available?
- Will they supply very small businesses?
- How soon do they require payment?
- Will they deliver? Delivery charges?
- History and reliability.
- Should you have more than one supplier for critical items especially at times of national emergency in light of say, Covid-19 or Brexit?
- Do you expect shortages or short-term delivery problems?
- Are supply costs steady or fluctuating? If fluctuating, how would you deal with changing costs?

Expenses/Overheads

Estimate costs as accurately as possible. It may be necessary to obtain quotes. If this is difficult, calculate probable costs based on findings for similar businesses/premises.

An explanation is needed for all expenses entered on your cash flow forecast. These costs are also needed in order to calculate overhead rates used in costing your product/service. They must be as accurate as possible.

Rent/rates	Details when premises found.
Heat/light	Estimate.
Advertising	Quotes from local press, magazines, Facebook and Google ads, etc.
Telephone	Installation costs plus estimated cost of calls.
Postage and stationery	Estimate your needs and obtain prices for business cards, etc.
Motor costs	Standard tax, get insurance quotes and estimate fuel and maintenance costs.

Insurance	Get quotes from brokers or online for insurance cover for equipment, employees, product and public liability, and any other necessary insurance.
Professional fees	Legal fees for property leases and accountants fees.
Wages	How many hours at what rate. Calculate cost of wages and salaries making sure to take into consideration National Minimum Wage and National Living Wage regulations or face the risk of expensive tax enquiries, fines and penalties.

Operations Outline

- Production.
- Equipment.
- Location.
- Costs.
- Legal environment.
- Personnel.
- Inventory.
- Suppliers.
- Expenses and overheads.

Complete your own Operations section by using the outline above. This is also downloadable from www.amci-associates.co.uk/succeed/

SECTION 8.   LEGAL ISSUES

'If you must break the law, do it to seize power: in all other cases observe
it.'
Julius Caesar – Roman General

Income Tax and the Small Business

Unless you are operating in a tax haven, taxes are just part of life for any
business usually administered by the tax authorities in the country of your
choice. In the UK, H M Revenue and Customs is the department that deals
with income tax. Refer to www.hmrc.gov.uk.

Income and other taxes are an area that is usually taken care of by an
accountant. It is important to work with an accountant from an early stage so
that the business is registered within the deadlines set by the tax authorities
and appropriate amounts of taxes are paid in a timely manner to avoid the
interest and penalties that can be charged otherwise.

Sole Traders - Starting Up

People who are intending to set up in business in the UK are required to
notify the tax office within three months of starting the business.

What Records to Keep

A simple, methodical system is more important than a complicated,
sophisticated one. For many small businesses a few simple accounts books
may well be sufficient:

- A sales book to record each sales transaction.

- A purchases book to record details of all purchases (date, supplier,
  amount, when paid, etc).

- A record of all cash transactions is also needed.

- A record must be made of all fixed assets purchased, i.e. buildings,
  machinery, vehicles, etc.

- A record of all stock.

Much of the above is done using bookkeeping software such as Intuit
QuickBooks, Xero, Sage, FreeAgent and other software providers. Many of
these are very popular software providers worldwide. In the UK, it is

important to be digitally compliant under the HMRC Managing Tax Digital (MTD) project. This information is required in order to calculate net profit, which is taxable. It is possible to claim many business expenses before net profit is calculated.

Checklist of Expenses

1 General Expenses

Cost of stock/materials

Selling costs (e.g. advertising)

Office/factory expenses (heat, light, etc.)

Travel, motor, trade journals, professional fees.

2 Staff Costs

Wages, salaries (but not your own salary)

National Insurance contributions (but not your own)

Some other staff costs.

3 Financial Expenses

Bank charges

Interest on loans and overdrafts for business

Business insurance.

4 Some Legal and Other Expenses

Businesses can also get tax relief on capital expenditure (e.g. buying fixed assets such as plant and machinery).

When Income Tax is Payable

At the end of the first year's trading it is necessary for a Profit and Loss Account to be prepared and the business will pay tax on its profit for the year. It may not be required to pay this tax for some months and then it is payable in two parts; the first part by 31st January and the second part the following July.

For the second year of trading, tax is paid on the profit made during year one or year two depending on the accounting year end date.

Partnerships

The taxable income for a partnership is worked out in much the same way as for a sole trader, i.e. deducting expenses allowable for tax purposes, from the sales figure.

There are some differences however regarding the way the HMRC divides the profits between partners. For this reason it is essential to have a clear written partnership agreement that states how partners intend to divide up the tax bill.

Limited Companies

Tax for a limited company is called 'corporation tax'. The way the amount of income and gains is worked out is much the same as for a sole trader or partnership, however, certain differences do occur such as the timing of tax payments, tax assessment, the way wages/drawings are treated, involvement of National Insurance, etc.

N.B. It is essential that your cash forecast takes account of your estimated expenditure for tax payments so that the cash is there when needed, although the actual payments are not usually made until well into year two.

At AMCI, regardless of your business model, we can advise you on all aspects of personal and business taxation. We can assist you to minimise your taxes using established strategies ensuring you can achieve your financial freedom much sooner. We can also incorporate the private limited company making sure that it is done properly and efficiently to start your business. If you are to adopt a private limited company structure, you must incorporate the company before attempting to open the business bank account. These days, high street banks are very reluctant to invite customers to the branch and therefore, try setting-up the bank account online. Most high street banks and challenger banks, such as Tide, Starling, and Counting-Up, have user friendly online facilities for you to set this up.

Employing Other People

If a business employs other people, it is the responsibility of the owner to administer the income tax payments of his/her employees through the PAYE system. Much of this is done electronically by deploying computerised software packages such as Brightpay or QuickBooks. These days, payroll is processed in real time usually either weekly or monthly. Make sure to keep records of hours worked by staff, time off for breaks, and holidays taken. In the case of a visit by HMRC, these will be required or may incur unnecessary costs and penalties.

National Insurance

National Insurance (NI) payments act as a form of social security, since the payment of NI contributions establishes entitlement to certain state benefits for workers and their families.

Currently, employers pay contributions for each worker from the age of sixteen years, until the age they become eligible for the state pension.

Contributions are also due from employed persons earning at or above a threshold called the Lower Earnings Limit, the value of which is reviewed each year. Self-employed persons contribute partly through a fixed weekly or monthly payment, and partly on a percentage of net profits above a threshold, which is reviewed periodically. Contributions are collected by HMRC.

There are four classes of NI contribution, Classes 2 and 4 are payable by self-employed people. Class 1 is for employees and Class 3 is voluntary.

Please refer to the HMRC (www.hmrc.gov.uk) website for the latest rates on National Insurance contributions.

VAT (Value Added Tax)

VAT is a tax charged on the 'supply of goods or services in the United Kingdom'. It is also charged on imported goods. We have seen worked examples earlier during the pricing section.

There are two categories of goods:

1 Exempt VAT is not chargeable on these items and therefore a supplier of these goods/services cannot reclaim any VAT paid. Examples: MOT on vehicles, insurance, financial services.

2 Rated these items can be charged at either standard rate which is currently 20 percent (most goods such as professional services, luxury goods), or zero rate (e.g. children's clothing, books), depending on the type of goods/service. Fuel, e.g. gas, electricity and oil, is currently charged at 5 percent.

Who Collects VAT?

Registration with HMRC is a legal requirement if you are supplying either zero-rated or standard-rated goods/services and if your past or expected future sales exceed the statutory limits. Refer to www.hmrc.gov.uk.

It is important to seek registration at the right time for the following reasons:

1 To avoid penalty payments for non-registration.

2 To recover VAT on setting up costs and other costs.

Accounting records have to be kept for a minimum of six years.

VAT Returns

Information relating to your sales and purchases has to be submitted, usually on a quarterly basis to HMRC digitally under MTD regulations. At AMCI, we can assist with choosing the most suitable software options in order to make your business as efficient as possible. There are many software providers, however, our platinum partner, 'Intuit QuickBooks', is the market leader in the UK and we can obtain the necessary software at a discounted price to keep your costs down.

Penalties

Penalties can be imposed by the HMRC for the following reasons:

1 Late registration

2 Late submissions

3 Late payment of VAT due.

Other

VAT officers can visit your business at any time after registration to carry out the check of your business records. In order to minimise risks of visits, it is important to prepare your VAT returns accurately and submit them on time.

Business Law

Laws are an important aspect of all forms of business activity. Whilst all businesses are subject to the law in the same way as individuals, certain aspects have a direct effect on businesses.

The Law of Contract

This is the foundation of commercial law. A contract is an agreement, with several specific requirements, that is enforceable by law.

The Law of Tort

This covers civil wrongs and includes negligence, for example if a manufacturer of foodstuffs supplied a contaminated product, the breach of duty of care to the consumer could result in legal proceedings.

Insurance

There arc two different categories of business insurance:

- Insurances you must have by law.
- Insurances you could consider to cover risks and disasters.

Insurance you must have:

Employers' Liability

You must have insurance to pay out for your liability if one of your employees is injured or ill as a result of working for you.

Motor Insurance

Motor insurance is required for businesses as for individuals, but you may need to pay an extra sum to cover your vehicle for business use.

Insurance Needed by Contracts

Some contracts, e.g. lease or hire purchase agreements, require you to obtain insurance.

Engineering Equipment Insurance

The law requires that certain equipment, e.g. pressure vessels, are checked and passed as safe at regular intervals. Maintenance can be combined with an insurance policy to cover against risk of explosion.

Other insurance to consider:

Public Liability and Product Liability

This will cover your liability if your business causes injury or illness to a member of the public or damage to their property. Product liability insurance covers you for risks which occur as a result of the product that you are producing or selling.

Insurance Against Fire and Other Perils.

Covers destruction or damage by fire, storm, etc.

Insurance for Loss of Profits

Could be important if fire or other disaster destroys work premises so business cannot continue for a time.

Insurance against Theft

This covers loss of or damage to the contents of your premises caused by theft. Cover for loss of cash is often extra.

Professional Indemnity

If the end product of a business is giving expert advice then this insurance can cover against claims from a client for damages caused by negligence or misconduct.

There are many other sorts of insurance to cover other possible business situations, including:

- Credit insurance.
- Goods in transit.
- Legal expenses.
- Window insurance.
- Computers and computer records.

Employment Law

This involves:

- Provision of a contract of employment by employers to employees.
- Awareness of employees' statutory rights.
- Conditions of employment.

Health and Safety

Employers are responsible for ensuring that workers are protected against all reasonable risks including:

- Safe handling of dangerous substances, precautions necessary for safe operation of machinery, etc.
- Working conditions - legislation requires employers to provide adequate light, heat, ventilation, etc.
- Welfare - most firms seek to provide for the wellbeing of their employees by the provision of various facilities.

Many businesses also require planning permission for various activities, such as fast food outlets and restaurants. There are many other business activities requiring licences from Borough or District Councils, e.g. music and dancing, cinemas, pet shops, scrap metal, etc.

Intellectual Property

Intellectual property consists of your brand name, inventions, the design work and things you write, make or produce. Copyright, patents, designs and trade marks are all types of intellectual property. For some of these, you get automatic protection, others you have to apply for to prevent other people from stealing your ideas. The Intellectual Property office can guide you here: www.gov.uk/government/organisations/intellectual-property-office.

General Data Protection Regulation (GDPR)

It is vitally important that any data held by the organisation is compliant with the General Data Protection Regulation (GDPR). It determines what information you can collect, how long you can hold it and what you can do with it. Many aspects of the business can be impacted by GDPR and creating a GDPR policy for the data you wish to collect and store will ensure that new staff will have a guideline which keeps them and your business inside of the law. Further guidance is available at www.gdpr-info.eu and www.ico.org.uk.

Legal Issues Outline

- Checklist of expenses.
- Records to keep.
- Handling income tax.
- Employing other people.
- Handling VAT.
- Insurance needed and costs.
- Employment law requirements.
- Intellectual Property issues.

You can now complete your Legal Issues section by using the outline above. This is also downloadable from www.amci-associates.co.uk/succeed/

CASE EXAMPLE – BUN & PERI (www.bunandperi.co.uk)

Having worked in the fast food outlets for a number of years, the proprietor approached me with the view of setting up a fast food business during the early days of the Covid-19 pandemic. I had advised him that before he decides to embark on the entrepreneurial journey, it was important to construct a plan of action that will allow him to fulfil his goal. Work was started on the business plan that included setting up the company, creating a bank account with one of our collaborative partner banking institutions, Starling Bank, and registering the name with the Intellectual Property Office. All of these services were carried out by AMCI to ensure that the business gets off the ground successfully.

Once the appropriate location was found, a food hygiene licence was obtained from the council and a lease agreement was signed with an appropriate break out clause to minimise risk. Refurbishment was done within three months ensuring that the image created reflected the long term objectives of turning the enterprise into a viable franchise operation. Fixtures, fittings and equipment were obtained after taking quotes from at least three different suppliers for each type of fixed asset. The suppliers selected were the ones that could supply the fixed assets both within the time frame and cost effectively.

The seating area was laid out to create ambiance and to ensure food could be consumed reasonably quickly to increase a quick turnaround of customers—there was no other similar setting within three mile radius serving the peri peri chicken experience. The menu was carefully crafted with dishes tested for taste and texture by adopting scientific management principles. Workflow in the kitchen was systemised to ensure food was prepared efficiently. Processes, procedures and systems were established so that the concept could be easily replicated as a possible franchise as per the business plan devised earlier.

All staff hired had previous fast food experience and training was provided by the proprietor to ensure that they understood the Bun & Peri concept. Business insurance was taken up to cover employer, public and product liability.

Due to the Covid-19 pandemic, the takeaway system using Uber Eats and self-employed drivers was launched in November 2020 with great success. The use of leaflets in the locality, the creation of a website, and a social media strategy has worked well so far. Once the pandemic is over, the restaurant area will be fully utilised leading to a great deal of further success. Reviews so far have been excellent. AMCI will provide the full range of accountancy, taxation and business advisory services to ensure the business plan is fully implemented and that the objectives set out are achieved according to plan.

SECTION 9.   FINANCE

'Beware of little expenses; a small leak will sink a great ship.'
Benjamin Franklin – one of the Founding Fathers of the USA

Accounting

Accounting is the activity involved in the systematic recording and analysis of the financial affairs of a business.

The recording of business transactions (sales and purchases) is called bookkeeping.

The analysis and appraisal of the finances of a business or organisation is referred to as accounting.

Much of the above is done using computerised accounting systems such as Intuit QuickBooks to make the business more efficient and give them updated information, in some cases in real time. This improves decision making in the business; your Accountant can assist you here.

Reasons Why Accounts Are Needed

The accounts provide an information system from which decisions can be taken.

They provide a means by which past decisions can be evaluated and future strategies planned. They also provide an estimate of the value of the business.

Three important accounting records are:

- The Trading, Profit and Loss Account - a record of the business over the previous twelve months.
- The Balance Sheet - a snapshot of the business as it is now.
- The Cash Flow Forecast - a look to the future of the business.

In the business start-up phase, forecasts of these accounts help in providing the case for a lender to invest in your business. In creating financial projections for your business start-up, you will need to determine:

1. Projected spending and sales.
2. Financial projections.
3. Your financial needs in regards to borrowing finance.
4. Using these projections for planning.

5. Planning for contingencies.

6. Monitoring.

The accountant should take care of this function so that you can concentrate on running your own business. Also, regular financial reports can be provided by the accountant to highlight the progress of your business.

Projecting the Trading, Profit and Loss Account

The function of this account is to show whether the business has been making a profit and what the gross profit and net profit are. It is often prepared at the end of the business's financial year but it is useful to prepare it more often, e.g. quarterly.

Gross Profit

The difference between total sales and the cost of the materials/stock used in the products sold.

Net Profit

The cost of all overheads, e.g. rent, rates, heating, etc, is deducted from gross profit to calculate the net profit.

For service sectors, the trading account is not needed. Instead, the profit and loss account is sufficient to highlight the business activities.

Projecting the Balance Sheet

The balance sheet is a picture, taken at a particular point in the year (usually at the end of a business's financial year) of:

- What the firm owes - sources of capital used to purchase assets, and
- what the firm owns – resources, e.g. buildings, machines, stock, etc.

Sources of capital are known as liabilities. Resources are known as assets.

Liabilities

These can be long term or current.

Long term	Loans to the business over one year.
Current	Money owed to suppliers or short term loans payable within one year.
Capital	This is also a liability as it is owed by the business to

	the owner/owners of the business.
Retained profit	Profit from previous years trading retained in the business is a liability as it is owed to the business owners.

Assets

These can be fixed or current.

Fixed	Have a long life and are retained in the business, e.g. premises, machinery, vehicles, fixtures and fittings.
Current	Have a short life and will be used up in the course of trading activities and converted into cash within one year, e.g. stock of materials, stock of completed or part finished goods awaiting sale, money owed to the business (debtors) and cash in the bank.

Projecting the Cash Flow Forecast

A cash flow forecast is quite simply a record of when cash is expected to be received into the business and when it is expected to be paid out.

It is important that realistic assumptions are made about when cash is expected to be received and when and how much will be paid out. It is necessary to constantly seek reliable information upon which to base forecasts.

Sales figures and consequent sales income must be realistic and not over optimistic. Cash from sales may not be received for some time after actual sales are made. Costs must be investigated and estimated carefully and not pitched too low. Purchases for stock items should be in some way related to sales. Sales projections from the earlier section need to be included in the cash flow forecast.

The purpose of the forecast is to show what the business's needs for cash are at any particular time and therefore enabling it to plan funding requirements. The cash flow forecast is usually prepared for a year on a month-by-month basis.

Working Capital

Working capital is the money needed to finance the day to day running of the business. It pays the bills for stock and overheads (rent, electricity, telephone, etc.) as they fall due.

There is often a considerable time lapse between selling a product and subsequently receiving payment for it. Up to ninety days credit is the norm in some industries. A reserve of working capital bridges the gap between sales made and payment being received from customers.

Careful calculation of working capital requirements is needed in order that there are sufficient funds to meet financial commitments as they arise.

An estimate of future working capital requirements can be obtained by compiling a cash flow forecast.

A great deal of care and attention is needed when preparing the financial statements such as profit and loss, balance sheet and cash flow forecast. This is one area investors/lenders focus their attention on the most. Therefore, make sure you get this spot on. I have included examples that you can access at www.amci-associates.co.uk/succeed/.

Company Credit Policies

- Do you plan to sell on credit?

- Do you really need to sell on credit? Is it customary in your industry and expected by your clientele?

- If yes, what policies will you have about who gets credit and how much?

- How will you check the creditworthiness of new applicants?

- What terms will you offer your customers, i.e. how much credit and when is payment due?

- Will you offer prompt payment discounts? (Hint: Do this only if it is usual and customary in your industry.)

- Do you know what it will cost you to extend credit? Have you built the costs into your prices?

Budgeting

Budgeting is a means of business control. It is basically a plan which incorporates figures (e.g. sales, production, etc.) which you believe you may be able to achieve, and gives you and any employees something to aim for. The cash flow forecast is an example of a budget for a new business venture.

It is a mistake to include figures which are too easy to achieve in case the budget turns into an objective, rather than striving for the biggest profit possible.

To use the budget as a business control mechanism it is necessary to prepare it in advance, i.e. assemble next year's budget before the end of the current year, in order to avoid a time gap during which the business could drift. Others employed in the business should be involved in drawing up the budget forecasts for their particular areas of the business. This is necessary for a workable budget because it is useless to set sales forecasts that the production department cannot match with output or for which the marketing budget is inadequate.

How to Use the Budget

Actual cost, cash and profit figures need to be compared regularly with the forecast of budgeted figures in order to:

- identify what has gone right,

- identify what has gone wrong,

- decide what action to take to remedy any unfavourable differences, and

- identify problem areas for the future, which may only emerge over time as actual performance fails to keep up to budgeted performance.

Once the budget has been agreed upon by all the departments of the business, it is necessary to set up a system of management reporting. This should include reports on:

1. What has been achieved in the last period (probably a month) and how it compares with forecast performance objectives and figures, and highlighting reasons for success or failure.

2. What the outlook and specific objectives are for the following period.

As well as providing management information, it also provides employees with objectives and priorities, and enables them to monitor their performance.

Please see Appendix 5 for more details and a glossary on finance related terms.

SECTION 10. PRESENTING FINANCIAL FORECASTS IN YOUR BUSINESS PLAN

'Far and away the best prize that life offers is the chance to work hard at work worth doing.' *Theodore Roosevelt*

This important section in the business plan takes your work in Section 9 and uses it to show the financial viability of your business. It should be laid out as follows:

1. General Assumptions

Any assumptions made, for example in the remote environment.

2. Sales Forecast

Market research findings should confirm the possibility of obtaining these sales.

3. Start-Up Costs

These are costs incurred during the process of creating the business. Examples include the following:

- Costs of preparing the business plan.
- Research expenses.
- Arrangement fees for borrowing.
- Technological expenses such as cost of website, information systems and accounting software.
- Advertising and promotion.
- Employee expenses including recruitment and selection costs.
- Insurance, license and permit fees.
- Equipment and supplies.
- Accounting and legal costs including company formation fees.

4. Running Costs – day-to-day costs of operating the business. Refer to the Profit and Loss account example in the finance section of this book.

5.   Salaries and Contracts of Employees

6.   Funding Requirements

Total funding required, for example to cover start-up costs, fixed and current assets, and expenses. Often this is the short fall of funds necessary to launch the business venture.

This also involves a consideration of the Payback Period and Rate of Return

---

WORKED EXAMPLE – Fitness Geek Ltd.

Fitness Geek Ltd. needs to raise £125,000. This is to purchase the necessary machinery and vehicles to carry out essential maintenance on its equipment supplied to gymnasiums nationwide under the service agreements. It has projected the following cash flows and profits:

Year	Net Cashflow £	Net Profit £
1	45,000	34,500
2	57,500	36,850
3	58,750	38,500
4	38,500	38,950

Calculate the Payback Period and Accounting Rate of Return on this investment.

Payback is the amount of time taken to recover the initial investment using expected net cash flows, in this case of £125,000.

Year	Net Cashflow £	Cumulative Cashflow £
0	(125,000)	(125,000)
1	45,000	(80,000)
2	57,500	(22,500)
3	58,750	
4	38,500	

Therefore payback is 2 years and so many months.

Let's calculate the months below:

In year three, Fitness Geek Ltd. needs to recover £22,500 out of £58,750. Therefore, the number of months is:

(22,500/58,750) x 12 = 4.6 months. Round it to 5 months.

Payback period in this case is 2 years and 5 months.

Accounting Rate of Return (ARR) is average profits divided by initial investment and expressed in percentage terms. In the case of Fitness Geek Ltd. it is as follows:

$$\frac{34,500 + 36,850 + 38,500 + 38,950}{4}$$

$$\frac{37,200}{125,000} \times 100 = 29.8\% \text{ round it to } 30\%.$$

If all the assumptions hold for this venture, the rate of return seems attractive.

Activity 6: Calculate the payback period and accounting rate of return if the initial investment for Fitness Geek Ltd. was £161,250.

Solutions to Activity 6:

Fitness Geek Ltd.

Payback:

Year	Net Cashflow £	Cumulative Cashflow £
0	(161,250)	(161,250)
1	45,000	(116,250)
2	57,500	(58,750)
3	58,750	
4	38,500	

Payback period is exactly 3 years.

Accounting Rate of Return (ARR):

$$\frac{34,500 + 36,850 + 38,500 + 38,950}{4}$$

$$\frac{37,200}{161,250} \times 100 = 23.1\% \text{ round it to } 23\%.$$

You will also need to prepare:
- Three Year Cash Flow Forecast.
- Three Year Profit and Loss Forecast.
- Three Year Balance Sheet Forecast.

You may need the help of your accountant to do this.

Once finance has been approved you should be in the position to launch your business venture. Use Appendix 4 as a guide to the launch.

Presenting Financial Forecasts Outline

- Sales forecast.
- Start-up costs.
- Running costs – the day-to-day costs of operating the business.
- Salaries and contracts of employees.
- Forecast cashflow statement.
- Forecast balance sheet.
- Projected profit & loss account.
- Funding requirements.
- Payback period.
- Accounting rate of return.
-

You can now complete the Finance section by using the outline above. This is also downloadable from www.amci-associates.co.uk/succeed/

IHQLAK HUSSAIN

5 GAME PLAN FOR THE LAUNCH OF BUSINESS

'Plan for what it is difficult while it is easy, do what is great while it is small.' *Sun Tzu - Chinese philosopher*

'Success is not final; failure is not fatal: it is the courage to continue that counts.' – *Winston Churchill*

You have the business plan ready, acquired the necessary capital to invest, formulated a team and devised the marketing strategy to execute your business idea into action. Here are some practical steps that you need to take in order to launch your business.

Step 1: Register your business

Depending on the business model adopted, this is the birth of your business. If you are a sole trader or partnership, register your business with the tax authority. In the UK it is HMRC (www.hmrc.gov.uk). Apply for the licences and permits if required.

If your business is adopting a private limited company structure, you must incorporate the company and register it with the Registrar of Companies at Companies House. This is the legal process and it is better if you seek advice and have it done professionally by an accountant. You need to decide on the Registered Office, Company Director(s) and have proof of your identity ready including your home address that needs to be less than three months old.

Step 2: Set up your domain name and business email

Purchase the domain name. Keep the business email separate from personal email. Make it reflective of your business image.

.

Step 3: Protecting your idea

You want to stop people stealing your idea(s). The brand name, your inventions, the designs, and things you write are all important. Apply for protection with the Intellectual Property Office. This can take a while depending on the type of protection you are applying for. This is the reason why you often hear the phrase 'Protection Pending' from the entrepreneurs on the Dragons Den.

Step 4: Open a business bank account

This should only be done once step one has been completed. If you have formed the company, the company Certificate of Incorporation, Memorandum and Articles of Association are often requested together with the director(s) identification. This used to be a straightforward task but national emergencies such as Covid-19, Brexit, etc. have made it somewhat difficult, particularly with the high street banks. However, challenger banks that predominantly operate online such as Tide, Startling and Counting Up are more small business friendly.

Step 5: Maintain your business income and expenses

Record keeping is important. There are plenty of computerised software systems available for you to carry this step out effectively. Seek advice from your financial adviser such as AMCI as to which software to use.

Step 6: Content marketing plan

Produce the content, then decide how will you share your value proposition with your customers: online, off-line or a combination? Make sure to get this right from the start, seek feedback and testimonials from your customers. Set sales goals too. How many customers will you engage with, and how will you engage with them? For example, number of telephone calls, number of visits, number of clicks, number of followers on social media, etc.

Step 7: Create a website and implement your social media strategy

Set up a website including the landing page. In the 21st century, this is vitally important.

Step 8: Go for it!

In this book you have everything you need to set up your business. As I mentioned, this is for serious entrepreneurs only due to the amount of work, level of detail and sheer number of steps needed. Take your time, create your plan and get the necessary advice that you need. Should you work through these steps, you may find that you are one of the 98 percent of entrepreneurs that SUCCEED!

APPENDICES

Appendix 1
Business Start-Up Personality Test Outcomes

Do you have what it takes to succeed?

In order to succeed, you need to have certain traits and if you don't have them, you can always learn them. YOU need ideas, plan of action, a lot of patience and persistence, problem solving and good communication skills.

Thank you for completing the test. For every 'YES' response, award 4 points. Every 'NO' is worth 0 points. Total up your score. You will be classified into one of the following categories:

0 – 49 points

It doesn't sound like you are cut out to work on your own at this point in your life. You might be for someone else for now. Reconsider this when circumstances are more favourable. In the meantime, carry out plenty of reading on this subject matter including this book to develop your knowledge and understanding.

50 – 69 points

You seem to be lacking some of the qualities, attitudes or proper support. You need to develop your skills, attitudes and support mechanisms in the areas that you are lacking in. Perhaps, by taking on a partner that complements your skills, you can still do it. Read the book to find out what it takes to make a success of the enterprise journey.

70 – 84 points

You are certainly capable of making a business succeed! You might want to speak to several people (e.g. professionals such as an accountant, lawyer, etc.) beforehand and review some of the issues raised in your responses especially where you have answered 'No'. Read the book to improve your chances of success.

85 – 100 points

You are ready to embark on the entrepreneurial journey. It sounds like you have got the basic characteristics required for a successful beginning and long term survival. By reading this book, you will improve your experiences even further and chance to succeed!

Appendix 2
Sample Executive Summaries

PET GRANDMA INC.

Our Mission

Pet Grandma Inc. offers superior on-site pet sitting and exercising services for dogs and cats, providing the personal loving pet care that the owners themselves would provide if they were home. Our team will ensure that pet owners can take business trips or vacations knowing that their pets are in good hands.

The Company and Management

Pet Grandma Inc. is headquartered in the City of West Vancouver and incorporated in the Province of British Columbia. The company is owned by partners Pat Simpson and Terry Estelle. Pat has extensive experience in animal care while Terry has worked in sales and marketing for fifteen years.

The management of Pet Grandma Inc. consists of co-owners Pat Simpson and Terry Estelle. Both partners will be taking hands-on management roles in the company. In addition, we have assembled a board of advisors to provide management expertise. The advisors are:

1. Juliette LeCroix, partner at LeCroix Accounting LLP
2. Carey Boniface, veterinarian and partner at Little Tree Animal Care Clinic
3. John Toms, president of Toms Communications Ltd.

Our Services

Our clients are dog and cat owners who choose to leave their pets at home when they travel or who want their pets to have company when their owners are at work. Pet Grandma Inc. offers a variety of pet care services, all in the pet's home environment, including:

- Dog walking
- Daily visits
- 24-hour care for days or weeks
- Administration of medications by qualified staff
- Emergency treatment in case of illness (arranged through veterinarians)

- Plant watering
- Mail collection
- Garbage/recycling
- The market

Across Canada the pet care business has seen an explosion of growth over the last three years. West Vancouver is an affluent area with a high pet density. Our market research has shown that nine out of ten pet owners polled in West Vancouver would prefer to have their pets cared for in their own homes when they travel rather than be kenneled and six out of ten would consider having a pet sitter provide company for their dog when they were at work.

Our Competitive Advantages

While there are currently eight businesses offering pet sitting in West Vancouver, only three of these offer on-site pet care and none offers "pet visit" services for working pet owners.

Pet Grandma's marketing strategy is to emphasize the quality of pet care we provide ("a Grandma for your pet!") and the availability of our services. Dog owners who work, for instance, will come home to find happy, friendly companions who have already been exercised and walked rather than demanding, whiny animals.

All pet services will be provided by animal care certified staff.

All employees are insured and bonded.

Financial Projections

Based on the size of our market and our defined market area, our sales projections for the first year are $340,000. We project a growth rate of 10% per year for the first three years.

The salary for each of the co-owners will be $40,000. On start-up we will have six trained staff to provide pet services and expect to hire four more this year once financing is secured. To begin with, co-owner Pat Simpson will be scheduling appointments and coordinating services, but we plan to hire a full-time receptionist this year as well.

Already we have service commitments from over 40 clients and plan to aggressively build our client base through newspaper, website, social media, and direct mail advertising. The loving on-site professional care that Pet Grandma Inc. will provide is sure to appeal to cat and dog owners throughout the West Vancouver area.

Start-up Financing Requirements

We are seeking an operating line of $150,000 to finance our first-year growth. Together, the co-owners have invested $62,000 to meet working capital requirements.

This concludes the executive summary example based on the fictional company Pet Grandma Inc.

Source: https://www.thebalancesmb.com/business-plan-executive-summary-example-2948007

Appendix 3
Sample CV

Try to use no more than two pages.

Curriculum Vitae

Name; Address; Telephone number; Date of Birth; Status

Education Details
Schools/Colleges attended with dates
Subjects studied with dates
Grades/Qualifications obtained

Work Experience
Previous full or part time jobs, stating what they entailed and responsibilities with dates
Voluntary Work - type of work
Training Schemes attended
Any courses attended

State dates and names of employers including details of work carried out, skills learned, experience obtained. Stress skills that are relevant to your business idea.

Achievements
Hobbies and Interests
Any special hobbies or interests stating any skills and levels obtained.

It refers to anything you do which has a recognised qualification or level of responsibility with it, such as:
- Sports instructor – scuba diving, parachuting, skiing or snowboarding, rally driving, etc. – doesn't have to be extreme sports, just something which shows you hold a professional status and have responsibility for others and expertise within that field.
- St. John's Ambulance First Aid volunteer, steward at the Student's Union or a sporting venue – this shows you think of others, place safety first.

- Volunteering – if you volunteer in any capacity on a regular basis this shows your commitment to ours and your commitment to the process of giving to others which suggests you will demonstrate the same dedication to your business.

Name and addresses of at least two referees (note that to comply with GDPR you will need to get their permission first. Another option would be to state 'available on request').

Appendix 4
Designing Questionnaires

Do's	Don'ts
Start with a list of information that you require.	Ask for too much personal information.
Plan questions that will give you this information.	The information you do require should be asked at end of the interview?
Give a brief explanation of what the survey is about.	
Tell people you are not trying to sell anything.	Ask ages of interviewees - instead estimate it or provide wide age bands for them to choose appropriate band.
Make instructions absolutely clear.	Include too many questions - 12 to 15 maximum.
Group questions that are related.	
Provide simple system for recording answers, e.g. tick appropriate box.	Ask written questions – it's best to provide a selection of answers, as people only have to tick their choice.
Provide choice of answers.	
Carry out trial run - say 10.	Crowd the page layout.
Amend questionnaire if necessary after trial run.	Give confusing directions.
If you need a person's address or area where they live ask for the first part of their postcode - this should be sufficient. A full address is not needed and most interviewees are very reluctant to give this sort of information.	Use ambiguous terms, e.g. cheap or expensive - instead give specific examples, e.g.
	a) £5-£10
	b) £11-£20
	c) £21-£30.

Appendix 5
Glossary of Accounting Terms

Capital Invested

Money used to start a business, to buy equipment, buildings, vehicles, etc. This is the owner's own money and/or borrowed money or other assets introduced by the owner.

Working Capital

This is the money required in the business to meet bills for stock, overheads and other costs, as they fall due. There is usually a considerable time-lapse between the making and selling of a product and the receiving of payment for it. Working capital bridges that gap.

Cash flow

This is the flow of money coming into a business in receipts from customers and flowing out to suppliers and to pay for expenses. You need to work out this cash flow in advance so that the necessary amount of working capital is available to meet the business's needs. This is called a cash flow forecast.

Creditor

Somebody the business owes money to for goods or services supplied.

Debtor

A person/business who owes money to your business. A debt which is not paid and where there is little prospect of it even being paid is a 'bad debt'. Minimise bad debts by undertaking customer vetting.

Fixed Costs/Overheads

These are the costs of the business that remain the same regardless of how many items are produced. They cover things like rent, rates, insurance, telephone and stationery.

Variable Costs

Variable costs are associated with production of things, e.g. the materials that go into a product, so these costs vary with the number of products made.

Costing

To calculate the cost of making a product or providing a service it is necessary to include all the costs involved both fixed and variable to include,

i.e. Raw materials,

Labour,

Overheads.

Pricing

This is the process by which you calculate how much you will charge for your product. It will depend on materials used, labour time required and overhead costs. The prices of competitors' products will have to be taken into account before setting a selling price and other marketing considerations investigated.

Profit

This is the difference between total income from sales of the product and total expenditure incurred in the making and selling of the product.

Gross Profit

This is the difference between turnover (i.e. total sales of the business) and the cost of those sales (materials, bought in components).

Net Profit

This is calculated by taking gross profit and then deducting all overheads, e.g. rent, rates, lighting, administration costs, etc.

Profit and Loss Account

This is a statement of progress of the business over a twelve-month period and shows gross profit and net profit calculations.

Assets

Resources that are owned by the business. There are two main groups of assets: Fixed and Current.

Fixed Assets

Criteria for assets to be considered fixed:

1. The asset is expected to have a long life.

2. The asset is to be used in the business and is not for re-sale or conversion into cash.

Examples of fixed assets

- Land and buildings.
- Fixtures and fittings.
- Plant and machinery.
- Motor Vehicles.

Current Assets

Criteria for assets to be considered current:

- The asset is expected to have a short life.
- The asset is primarily used for conversion into cash.

Examples of current assets

- Stock - materials and/or finished products awaiting sale.
- Debtors - money owed to business.
- Bank balance.
- Cash in hand.

Liabilities

These are the sources of capital used to purchase assets.

Liabilities consist of:

- Money owed by the business for goods and services supplied.
- Money owed by the business to repay loans.
- Capital introduced by the owner to the business.

Therefore: Capital + Liabilities = Assets

Liabilities take several forms:

- Capital - money and value of equipment introduced into the business by the owner.
- Long term loans - loans to the business which do not require repayment in the near future.
- Current liabilities - money owed to suppliers by the business and short term loans.
- Retained profit - profit from previous years' trading kept in the business to invest.

Drawings

The money taken out of a business by the owner or partner for his or her own use.

(Only applicable for sole trader or partnerships.)

Balance Sheet

This is a statement which can provide a summary of the position of a business at any time but is usually prepared at the end of the business's financial year.

It shows the business's assets and liabilities, i.e. what the business owns or is owed, e.g. land, equipment, stock, etc, and where the capital came from to buy these assets, e.g. capital invested, loans, retained profit.

Break-Even

The break-even point is reached when the number of units of a product or service sold provides enough sales revenue to cover the total costs involved in their production, both fixed and variable. The break-even point represents the minimum number of units that must be sold to cover costs. At this point no profit is made.

Margins and Mark-Ups

Business people who are involved with retailing need to differentiate between these two concepts.

Margin

This is calculated using the relationship between Gross Profit and the Selling Price

i.e.   Selling Price - Buying Price x 100 = %

Selling Price

Mark-Up

This is calculated using the relationship between Gross Profit and the Buying Price

i.e.   Selling Price - Buying Price x 100 = %

Buying Price

Calculating the Selling Price of Your Product or Service

In order to calculate the selling price of your product or service, it is first necessary to find out how much it has cost to make or provide.

The costs involved in making a product can be divided basically into two groups:

Fixed Costs

There are certain basic costs (overheads) in any business such as:

- Salaries.
- Rent and rates.
- Insurance.
- Heating and lighting.
- Telephone.
- Stationery.
- Advertising.

All of these fixed costs must be taken into account when costing a product or service. These costs are not necessarily fixed forever but mostly can be predicted for the next twelve months.

Fixed costs have to be paid irrespective of whether a large or small number of products are made. Fixed costs do not vary directly with the volume produced.

Variable Costs

These costs vary directly with the number of units produced, as they are the direct costs of production:

- Materials/stock.
- Bought in parts.

Fixed Costs + Variable Costs = Total Cost of Production

The total cost of production (per unit) can be used as a starting point for setting the selling price.

It may be necessary to consider a range of selling prices for your product and to calculate the profit levels for each of these prices before deciding which selling price to use; however a price cannot be set in isolation, other market factors have to be considered, e.g. competitor's prices, image of product, etc.

It is essential to know how many units must be sold at a particular price to cover the total cost of production. This number is known as the 'break-even point'. Each unit sold in excess of the break-even point will contribute to a profit.

Example:

Consider these two possible selling prices for a wooden activity learning cube: £10.00 and £14.00.

The wooden activity learning cube is an interactive toy for child development. Kids will have hours of fun moving the brightly coloured beads along the winding and spiralling tracks. Ideal toy for developing hand-eye coordination as well as cognitive skills. The cube is manufactured using 100% FSC (Forest Stewardship Council) approved wood and water-based paint for safe play. The manufacturer needs to know how many cubes must be sold per week to cover the total cost of production.

Variable Costs for 1 cube = £3.50 (wood, glue, varnish, screws, etc.)

The Fixed Costs are £660.00 per week.

At £10.00 per cube:

Selling Price - Variable Cost = Contribution to Fixed Costs and Profit

So £10.00 - £3.50 = £6.50 - This is not profit as £660.00 fixed costs still have to be paid.

Each unit sold at £10.00 gives a contribution towards fixed costs of £6.50.

So fixed costs ÷ Contribution = Number of units to be sold to break-even.

£660.00 = 102 units must be sold per week to break-even.
£6.50

If 102 units are sold per week at £10.00 each then the total costs of production are covered - so this is the break-even point.

Every unit sold over 102 units per week will produce a contribution towards profit.

If 145 units are sold every week, the other 43 will contribute to profit.

At £14.00 per cube:

Selling Price - Variable Cost = Contribution to Fixed Costs and Profit

So £14.00 - 3.50 = £10.50 Contribution to fixed costs and profit.

Each unit sold at £14.00 gives a contribution towards fixed costs of £10.50.

Fixed Costs ÷ Contribution = Number of units to be sold to break-even.

£660.00 = 63 units need to be sold per week to break-even.
£10.50

Every unit sold over 63 units will contribute towards profits.

If sales of 145 units per week are made:

First 63 units needed to break-even therefore other 82 units will contribute to profit.

ABOUT AMCI

AMCI is a firm of accountants and management consultants that takes pride in providing a highly efficient service to all our clients locally and nationally.

In a dynamic environment, clients need to be confident that their financial affairs are in good hands. This confidence is gained by our friendly and personal approach to all professional matters and by the results achieved by our advice and recommendations.

We specifically focus on micro, small and medium sized businesses and taxpayers. Our experts have extensive experience in delivering a full range of accountancy, and business advisory services that keeps your business on the road to success.

We are proud of our service offerings; we therefore have established Management and Leadership development training division. This division consists of tutors with many years of international experience. We are not your traditional training provider as we pride ourselves on our pragmatic delivery style and the realism we place on the challenges faced by today's executives.

Our result-focused approach means we build strong, long lasting relationships with our clients. AMCI works with their clients to support them meet their aims and aspirations. In doing so, we will save you time, assist you to gain greater returns on investment and minimize risks.

We will support you now and in the future, and give you complete peace of mind. We offer bespoke service delivery. If there is anything you need, feel free to just ask us!

For all of our services please visit www.amci-associates.co.uk.

FURTHER READING AND RESEARCH

We have devised a comprehensive business start-up course to assist you further with all aspects of starting up a business venture. To find out more, contact us at info@amci-associates.co.uk.

Books

Blokdyk G (2020) Innovation. A Complete Guide, Emereo Publishing

Davies B (2020) Your Business Your Way, Discover Your Bounce Publishing

Jenkins R (2019) Winning Big in Sales, Discover Your Bounce Publishing

Knight P (2016) Shoe Dog: A Memoir by the creator of NIKE, Scribner Book Company

Longenecker J et al (2016) Small Business Management: Launching & Growing Entrepreneurial Ventures 18th Ed, Centag Learning

Stoke d & Wilson N (2021) Small Business Management & Entrepreneurship 8th Ed, Pearson

Useful Journals and Websites:

We would be delighted to advise and guide you as you start your business and also work with existing micro, small and medium-sized businesses. Read more and contact us through our website: www.amci-associates.co.uk/succeed/.

Accounting and Legal: www.companieshouse.gov.uk www.hmrc.gov.uk www.accaglobal.com www.aat.org.uk www.acas.org.uk To Collect Market Research: www.surveymonkey.co.uk	Further Reading: www.economist.com www.oecd.org www.wto.org www.gemconsortium.org

Printed in Great Britain
by Amazon